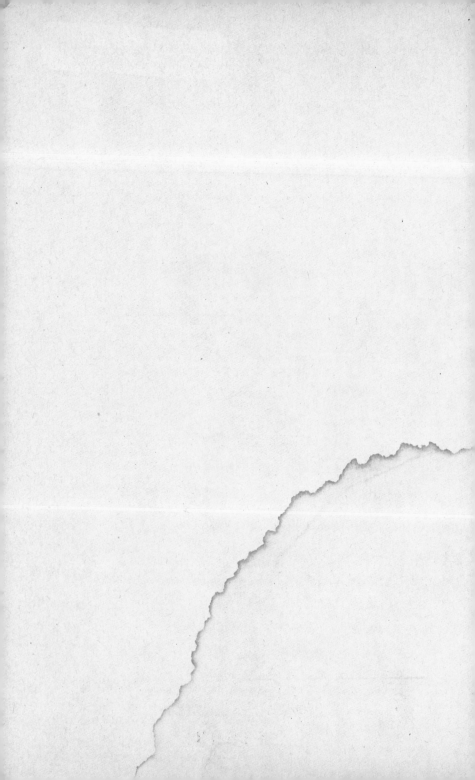

SHOULD
I GET
MARRIED ?

M. Blaine Smith

INTERVARSITY PRESS
DOWNERS GROVE, ILLINOIS 60515

InterVarsity Press is the book-publishing division of InterVarsity Christian Fellowship, a student movement active on campus at hundreds of universities, colleges and schools of nursing. For information about local and regional activities, write Public Relations Dept., InterVarsity Christian Fellowship, 6400 Schroeder Rd., P.O. Box 7895, Madison, WI 53707-7895.

Distributed in Canada through InterVarsity Press, 860 Denison St., Unit 3, Markham, Ontario L3R 4H1, Canada.

All Scripture quotations, unless otherwise indicated, are from the Holy Bible, New International Version. Copyright © 1973, 1978, International Bible Society. Used by permission of Zondervan Bible Publishers.

Cover photograph: Michael Goss

ISBN 0-87784-1730-1

Printed in the United States of America ∞

Library of Congress Cataloging-in-Publication Data

Smith, M. Blaine.
    Should I get married?/M. Blaine Smith.
        p.   cm.
    ISBN 0-8308-1730-1
    1. Marriage—Religious aspects—Christianity.   I. Title.
BV835.S585   1990
248.4—dc20   90-32638
                                                                              CIP

13   12   11   10   9   8   7   6   5   4   3   2   1
99   98   97   96   95   94   93   92   91   90

*This book is dedicated
to my wife, Evie, and our sons,
Benjamin and Nathan,
who are a constant reminder to me
of God's grace
in creating families.*

I
Setting
Your
Sights

1
The Search
for
Perspective

Most of the happily married couples I know confess that the road to finding the right person was a rocky one at best. There were many false starts and disappointments along the way, and there was even a lot of confusion in reaching the decision they finally made. One very happily married woman in her late forties admitted to me in all honesty, "If I were widowed, I don't think I could go through the process of finding a husband again."

I do know a Christian couple who were acquainted only four days before becoming engaged. The decision to marry involved no struggle for either of them. Though only in their young twenties, they were each mature enough to make a wise choice. They've been married over fifteen years now and have had an exemplary relationship. They show that whatever may be said about the challenge of choosing a marriage partner, or the need for a long acquaintance period, there are exceptions to every rule.

I'm hard-pressed, though, to think of another example like theirs. My own odyssey toward marriage definitely fit the rule and not the exception. I was painfully shy as an adolescent and teen-ager. While I did enjoy a dating relationship in my young teens which lasted over a year, several others which I longed to initiate never got off the ground. Things began to improve after I gave my life to Christ at age nineteen. My social confidence in general increased remarkably.

By the time I was twenty-five, however, I'd been through three relationships where my expectations were seriously disappointed. In one I even believed I'd received a revelation from God that we would marry, which in time proved to be so much wishful thinking. In another, all the signposts seemed to indicate marriage, and we enjoyed a good relationship for a year and a half. Yet in time we discovered our vocational goals were so different as to make marriage untenable. Following a seminar that left me guilt-ridden for wanting marriage so much, I even resolved to forsake dating for a semester. While some important benefits came from this time, I realize now that my motives for this temporary vow of singleness were less than healthy.

Things took a very encouraging turn when I was twenty-six and began dating Evie Kirkland. We were married within a year! In the end God's grace triumphed over my own blundering and confusion as it always does. Yet, I must confess I felt like a ship lost at sea without a compass for much of this time. I know that much of the pain and poor judgment I had before this could have been eliminated if I'd had better instruction on how to choose a life partner.

Some Common Concerns

So many Christian singles have told me they are frustrated or confused in dealing with relationships and the question of marriage that I suspect my own experience with deciding to marry is the rule and not the exception today. There are a variety of points at which many feel adrift.

Married or single? Some are stuck at how to resolve the basic choice between marriage and singleness. We who are married can quickly forget what a complicated question this is for many singles, who hear different ideals about marriage and singleness being tossed around. Do you follow one of these ideals—and if so which one—or is it O.K. to simply follow your own preference? How do you find God's will in the midst of it all?

Getting off square one. Many others are quite comfortable with the idea of being married yet just as uncertain about how to get there. I know many bright, likeable singles well into their adult years who deeply want to be married but for various reasons have not been able to. A surprising number have never had a serious dating relationship at all.

Making the choice. Perhaps most surprising, though, is how many are in serious relationships yet unable to resolve whether to marry. The majority of those seeking my counsel in the last several years, in fact, have been looking for advice about whether to marry a particular person. Many of these are mature Christians with long-standing relationships, in which one or both cannot decide about marriage. In some cases the concern is over needing a clear sign from God. In others it's over whether one's ideals can be fully met in the relationship.

The fear of commitment. Still, some hesitate to marry from fears that marriage itself may be an overly confining or unpleasant experience. Not a few speak of commitment as claustrophobic—like being stuck in an elevator. A mature Christian woman admitted to me recently: "You know, I long for a relationship with a man, but when it finally becomes apparent that he wants to get serious I panic and want out. Once the relationship is over and the threat of commitment gone, I start liking him again." The fear of commitment not only causes some to bail out of perfectly good relationships but others to avoid dating altogether.

A map for the journey ahead. Finally, there are many who, while not overly concerned about getting married at this point, would like some perspective on how to move toward marriage at some time in the future. Unfortunately, they too often end up frustrated, for little meaningful direction on this matter is given by the church today. Among the many churches with which I'm acquainted, only one has a course in finding a spouse. And little of substance has been written on the subject by Christian writers.

Encouragement and Direction

Which brings me to the purpose of this book. Increasingly, I've wanted to put something in print which would give some navigational direction to those at each of these points of need and spiritual encouragement as well. I intend this to be a guidebook for working through the major stages in considering marriage. I want to offer counsel for choosing between marriage and singleness, seeking a compatible relationship, judging your compatibility with someone else, and dealing with commitment fears. My interest is fueled especially by remembering how helpful it would have been to me to have had a volume of this sort available as a young believer.

Three Blind Spots

When I reflect on my experience as a single Christian, I'm struck by two things. First, I'm certain that some of the difficulties I experienced were unavoidable. There is a mystery—in short, a risk—in human relationships that can never be avoided if we are to experience the adventure of life as God has designed it and move toward the goal of an intimate lifetime relationship.

Yet I also realize only too well that some of my problems resulted from certain well-intentioned, but misguided, perspectives which made me prone to bad judgment and a sitting duck for disappointment. In my work with singles today I find these same unfortunate viewpoints coming up again and again, and the problems that result are all too predictable. They tend to fall under three general areas:

One is *spiritualizing*. By "spiritualizing" I mean expecting an unreasonable measure of guidance from God. Scripture shows that while God graciously guides our decisions, he seldom eliminates the need for us to think them through and ultimately take responsibility for resolving them. Yet, many Christians expect him to guide in a mystical or supernatural fashion which would supersede this process and remove all personal responsibility.

The belief leaves some Christians uneasy about taking any personal initiative in finding a marriage partner. Others who are in serious relationships feel compelled to wait for an unmistakable sign from God before finally deciding to marry. And some are too quick to think God has given them a revelation to marry through some inner feeling or ironic coincidence. They don't do the hard work of carefully thinking the decision through.

Similar problems are caused by *idealizing*. This occurs when we hold to unreasonable ideals about romantic love or the perfect mate. Having ideals for marriage is crucial, but it is vital that these be realistic and in line with God's best intentions for our lives. In reality the influence of both our secular and Christian cultures is such that few of us enter adulthood without the need for some revising—often drastic—of our ideals before we will be in a position to find a suitable mate or make healthy decisions about marriage.

Many fail to see the marriage potential in a good relationship because their partner (or their feeling of romantic love) falls short of some unreasonable ideal. Others are too quick to think they have found the perfect companion in someone who seems to match up to certain stereotypes.

There is a third mindset that can be just as great an obstacle to sound decision making as the first two, which I term *catastrophizing*. (Yes, I invented the word; the English vocabulary doesn't provide a verb meaning "excessive worrying about the future.") By catastrophizing I mean harboring unreasonable fears of risk or change by dwelling on problems that are not likely to occur or obsessing over the possibility of making a wrong decision. There are a variety of fears which one normally experiences in taking steps toward marriage, ranging from the fear of rejection to the fear of decision making to the fear of commitment itself.

Some fear is healthy in a step as major as marriage, for it causes you to take the decision seriously and spurs you to trust more fully in Christ. But excessive fear can hinder clear thinking about marriage and keep you from going ahead when a suitable opportunity presents itself. Without some willingness to risk, indeed without a proper sense of adventure, you will never take the plunge into marriage.

Throughout the book I'll look at misleading ideas that arise in each of these three areas and how they can get you off track at different stages of considering marriage. I'll draw on examples from my own life and the experiences of others whom I've known and counseled. At each point I'll do my best to point you to outlooks which I understand to be more in line with Scripture and healthy thinking.

My hope is that this book will benefit you in three major ways:

☐ In helping you clarify how Christ's responsibility and your own relate in decisions about marriage.

☐ In helping you establish healthy ideals about marriage, singleness and who you would consider marrying.

☐ In giving you perspective on how to deal with fears that may be keeping you from God's best in these areas.

Our Task Ahead

I have structured this book to help you work through the issues involved in making a marriage decision. We will look first at the question of choosing between marriage and singleness (chapter two). Because this is foundational to everything else considered in this book, I want to begin by offering clear counsel for thinking this issue through.

In part two we will take a close look at God's guidance in our lives, especially as it touches decisions related to marriage. While I stress God's role in finding a spouse and the vital need for faith and trust on our part, I also examine some common misconceptions about how the Lord guides our decisions. These can keep you from taking proper responsibility for finding a mate or from clear thinking when it comes to making a decision about marrying someone.

Part three is the heart of the book. It provides perspective for deciding whether to marry once you're in a serious relationship. I offer guidelines for assessing your compatibility with another person, your readiness for marriage and whether the balance of factors add up to a decision for marriage.

My purpose in part four is to give encouragement to those who are eager to find a serious relationship. Steps are suggested which can help you find and develop a relationship with prospects for marriage.

Finally, in part five I examine the fear of commitment, looking at problems caused by it and recommending ways to deal with them. I discuss how to recognize this fear in yourself or someone else, how to respond to someone who is afraid of commitment and, if this fear is a problem for you personally, what steps you can take to overcome it.

You may wonder why the section on finding a serious relationship follows the one on weighing compatibility instead of preceding it. It might seem more logical to talk first about how to gain a quality relationship and then about how to judge whether it is fit for marriage, rather than the other way around. Let me assure you that there is a method to my madness.

Determining what it is you are looking for in a relationship is a vital first step toward finding one. I often find that singles who are eager for marriage harbor unrealistic ideals which are hindering them from finding someone who really would be suitable for them.

In fact clarifying your expectations can simplify the search for a mate, sometimes considerably. Some even find that they already know someone who would make an excellent spouse—perhaps a close friend—whom they've overlooked because their expectations were unreasonable. While this may or may not be true in your case, I do want to urge you first to read part three (and the sections preceding it) before moving to part four.

I would also like to mention that while I cite many real-life incidents throughout the book, I've changed incidental details and gender in some cases in order to protect the identities of those involved. I've also felt free to combine and create examples to illustrate particular points.

Staying Hopeful

Finally, let me mention that my experience not only gives me empathy for the struggles of single Christians but an important basis for extending hope as well. For one thing, my ministry has brought me into contact with many who are truly contented and joyful in the single life. I've been reminded many times of how God gives grace and fullness of life to those who are single. If your calling is to stay single, I hope you will take considerable encouragement from the discussion ahead.

I've often been impressed, too, with how God can work miracles to bring two people together in a lifetime union. I share the awe of a couple I recently married, who felt it remarkable that they grew up 3,000 miles apart, in radically different circumstances, yet through the providence of God met and decided to marry.

My own experience as a single Christian has taught me the significance of certain changes in perspective, and this more than anything inspired me to write this book. As my thinking changed at several important points, my journey toward marriage progressed as well. The result has been sixteen years of a happy, fulfilling marriage. I've seen this pattern repeated time and again for many I've known who at one point were ready to give up but now are in happy, solid marriages.

I say this cautiously, for—in spite of the preposterous claims of some popular titles—no book can guarantee that you will find a marriage partner. Yet I do believe that the perspectives presented in this book can improve your prospects—perhaps considerably—by helping you to be most fully open to the abundant provision of Christ for your life.

I write this book in a highly optimistic and hopeful spirit! I hope that will be contagious in the pages ahead.

2

Does God
Want Me to
Be Married
or Single?

▰▰▰▰▰

Has God created me to be a married person or am I in fact better suited for staying single? In which state will I be most fulfilled? In which will I best serve Christ? How can I know which is God's will for me?

Before we can talk about principles for choosing a mate or guidelines for building a serious relationship, we need first to consider the more fundamental question of choosing between marriage and single life. The question is important not only for those who are unattached and wondering how to direct their energies, but also for those in serious relationships who are confused about whether to forsake the single life for marriage.

Fortunately, Scripture speaks to this issue in a clear and liberating way. Unfortunately, this is an area where Christians are especially prone to unhealthy idealizing. The balanced message of Scripture is often overshadowed by idealized perspectives which are assumed to be biblical. This idealizing is at the root of most of the confusion which Christians experience in choosing between marriage and the single life. There are three common ways it happens.

"Married or Buried"

Some Christians idealize marriage. Some even go as far as to regard it as an almost universal need. Though it's seldom said explicitly, there's an underlying assumption in many churches and Christian groups that marriage is a more healthy state than singleness. While this creates a comfortable climate for those who want to pursue marriage, it wreaks havoc for those who either cannot find a mate or wish to remain unattached.

In *Single and Whole* Rhena Taylor documents her struggle to accept herself as a single woman among friends who feel she is missing something essential to life. Rhena is a contented single. As an energetic and creative missionary, she enjoys the freedom of being unattached. No matter how deeply she looks into herself, she cannot find a gaping need waiting to be filled by a husband and family.

Yet friends console her for being without a mate. They read feelings into her that simply aren't there. They tell her in subtle or not-so-subtle ways that she'd be happier and more effective married. Perhaps worst of all, she notes, "in over thirty years now as a Christian, I have never heard a minister of God preach on singleness as a good option for a Christian. I have sat through sermon after sermon after sermon on marriage but I have never heard a recommendation for the single state even though the pews have been filled with single people."[1]

She adds, "Could it be, I wonder, that the Western church has glorified marriage to such an extent that men and women who are truly called to the single state cannot stand up against the cultural and social emphases in society and so marry out of God's will? And, if that is so, what responsibility for that must be borne by the ministry of our Western church?"[2]

Rhena's point is sound. There is no question that many Christians overglamorize marriage. In many Christian circles those who opt for singleness do so at the cost of being regarded as second-class citizens. Others who are well-suited for single life are unfairly pressured toward marriage.

"Bachelors Till the Rapture"

I find, though, that the problem is often as great in the other direction. While some Christians idealize marriage, others do singleness. While no one would suggest that God wants all Christians to be single, there's a tendency in some Christian circles to think of the single life as a more virtuous state than the married.

Churches and parachurch ministries which place a high premium on missionary service often stress the special advantages of freedom which a single person has for such work. While some do this with a healthy sense of balance, others come off saying that the single person is actually in a better position than the married to serve the Lord as a missionary.

Singles ministries, seminars and books stress the benefits of singleness not only for those in missionary service, but for Christians in all walks of life. Again, while some do this with a proper respect for individual gifts and callings, others imply that the single person in general is following a higher calling than the one who settles for marriage.

Those who idealize the single life cite compelling biblical evidence for their position. Jesus and Paul, the two most significant personalities in the New Testament, were both single. And Paul spoke expressly of the benefits of the single life for devotion and service to the Lord in 1 Corinthians 7:32-34:

> I would like you to be free from concern. An unmarried man is concerned about the Lord's affairs—how he can please the Lord. But a married man is concerned about the affairs of this world—how he can please his wife—and his interests are divided. An unmarried woman or virgin is concerned about the Lord's affairs: Her aim is to be devoted to the Lord in both body and spirit. But a married woman is concerned about the affairs of this world—how she can please her husband.

There is no question that Paul saw special advantages in staying single. Yet those who idealize the single life tend to read these words in isolation from other statements Paul made which bring balance to his perspective.[3] Not a few Christians are drawn to the single life on the strength of these words alone, even when no one else is preaching the virtues of singleness to them.

Some Christians, like Rhena Taylor, are contented in the single state and enjoy the special benefits of being unattached. Like anyone, they go through periods of loneliness. Yet, generally, they are not preoccupied with thoughts of marriage and longings for a partner. They truly reflect the joyful single state which Paul talks about.

Some, though, who regard singleness as a higher calling, find it hard to bring their desires up to the level of their ideals. Underneath, they would strongly prefer to be married. Then if they do marry, they are nagged with the fear that they have settled for a less perfect will of God than they could have known. If they stay single, they consume a lot of energy dreaming about what marriage would be like. This often leads to self-deprecation and guilt for not being contented with God's "ideal," and the problem is compounded.

"I Don't Deserve to Be Married"

There's another reason that Christians opt for singleness, though, which has little to do with a high regard for single life. Some regard marriage as a prize so high that they assume they couldn't possibly be worthy of it. They look upon marriage as a reward which God gives to those who merit it through living an exemplary Christian life.

While this may seem a surprising viewpoint to those who don't identify with it, a number of serious Christians fall into it. They may believe that their behavior in past dating relationships or their fantasies about sex have been too ungodly to merit God's gift of marriage. Staying single becomes a form of self-punishment, a way of atoning for their own sins.

If those who think this way do marry, they may either be dogged with guilt or feel an unhealthy pride in having merited the "reward" of marriage. Typically, too, they hold a scrupulously high moral standard for the person they would consider marrying and are unforgiving of failings.

Not surprisingly, the basis of this perspective is often as much psychological as theological. Often those who hold it come from overly strict family backgrounds, where parents held them to an unfairly high standard, were unforgiving of their mistakes and withheld emotional support. As adults, this has caused them to withhold emotional rewards from themselves and others. Though they long for marriage on one level, they may sabotage the very possibility, through restricting their contacts or by breaking off any relationship which seems to have marriage potential.

I don't mean to imply that every Christian with the marriage-as-a-reward philosophy comes from a difficult family background. Some arrive at it simply through faulty reasoning. But whatever its basis, it squelches the motivation to seek marriage among some who most desire it. They assume that God's will must by definition be contrary to what they most deeply want.

The Biblical Perspective
Each of these idealized perspectives carries an element of biblical truth: God *does* will that most Christians eventually marry. Singleness *does* confer special advantages of grace for certain individuals. Mar-

riage *is* an extraordinary gift of God.

Yet each of these positions errs in taking the truth to an unhealthy extreme. There is no basis in Scripture for regarding either marriage or singleness as a more noble state in itself—it's always a question of God's will for an individual. And while marriage is a bountiful gift, it's never regarded in Scripture as a reward which one must merit.

When the biblical perspective on marriage and singleness is fully understood, it's found to be both balanced and liberating. It at once avoids the idealizing of the popular perspectives and gives us a succinct basis for deciding what our life's orientation should be. Perhaps most surprisingly, it puts the emphasis upon personal preference as the key to understanding God's will.

The biblical perspective can be summarized with several observations:

1. Marriage is given not because we deserve it, but because we need it. Scripture teaches that marriage, like salvation itself, is an unmerited gift from God. In the first reference to marriage in Scripture we read: "The LORD God said, 'it is not good for the man to be alone. I will make a helper suitable for him' " (Gen 2:18). Only one reason is mentioned for God bringing Eve into Adam's life—the fact that Adam needed companionship. Nothing is said about Adam deserving a wife, nor is it even suggested that Adam would serve God better with a spouse. It's simply said that Adam had a personal need, and this was basis enough for God to fill the void.

Several verses later it becomes clear that Adam and Eve reflect God's intentions for humanity in general. "For this reason a man will leave his father and mother and be united to his wife, and they shall become one flesh" (Gen 2:24). Just as Adam and Eve were brought together because of their mutual need, so God deems that others will be led by their own companionship needs to seek a spouse.

Paul reiterates the point in 1 Corinthians 7:1-7, in light of our inherent need for sexual fulfillment. One would have to read this passage with blinders on to miss its explicit message:

Now for the matters you wrote about: It is good for a man not to marry. But since there is so much immorality, each man should have his own wife, and each woman her own husband. The husband should fulfill his marital duty to his wife, and likewise the wife to her husband. The wife's body does not belong to her alone but also to her husband. In the same way, the husband's body does not belong to him alone but also to his wife. Do not deprive each other except by mutual consent and for a time, so that you may devote yourselves to prayer.

Then come together again so that Satan will not tempt you because of your lack of self-control. I say this as a concession, not as command. I wish that all men were as I am. But each man has his own gift from God; one has this gift, another has that.

In graphic language Paul says that marriage is a gift to help us avoid the inclination toward sexual immorality. Our idealistic mindset would expect Paul to say, "Since there is so much immorality, you must first prove yourself morally worthy to be married." Or, "Since there is so much immorality, you must avoid marriage, since it would indulge your sexual appetite." But to the contrary, Paul sees marriage as an antidote to sexual impurity.

Paul puts aside the philosophy which says that marriage is a reward for personal righteousness. To those who hold that philosophy, Paul would say: "Yes, you're correct in saying you don't deserve to be married. Who deserves *any* of God's gifts? Yet you may well *need* to be married. If you do, and you have a suitable opportunity, you will better honor Christ by marrying. To choose not to marry in this instance would amount to choosing to live the Christian life through your own strength rather than accepting God's provision of grace."

2. *Celibacy is a gift given to some, but not all.* Paul's language clearly indicates that most Christians will best serve Christ through getting married: "each man should have his own wife, and each woman her own husband." Paul, however, stops far short of the popular philosophy which idealizes marriage and views it as a universal need. He

also extols the benefits of the single life, beginning 1 Corinthians 7 with the statement "It is good for a man not to marry," then referring to his own enjoyment of the single life (v. 7), and finally noting explicitly how being single frees you from certain burdens that inevitably come from being married (vv. 32-35).

Crucial to understanding Paul's perspective on singleness, though, is the fact that he regards the ability to live contentedly unmarried as a spiritual gift. "Each man has his own gift from God; one has this gift, another has that" (v. 7). Later in 1 Corinthians Paul has an extensive discussion on spiritual gifts (chaps 12-14). From this three points come across that are important to understanding his attitude toward singleness:

a. No Christian has all the spiritual gifts. Each believer is given only those gifts that manifest God's unique purpose for his or her life (1 Cor 12:4-7).

b. No one can obtain a spiritual gift they don't already possess simply by striving for it, as Paul's analogy of gifts in the body of Christ to parts of the human body (1 Cor 12:14-31) vividly demonstrates. Just as a toe cannot decide to become an eyelid, so one with the gift of administration cannot suddenly decide to discard that gift and take on the gift of preaching. You either have a spiritual gift or you don't.

The same point applies to the gift of singleness. It's a gift provided by God to some but not others. If God hasn't given it to me, there's no way I can attain it, anymore than one without a gift of music can expect that practice will enable them to inspire others through their singing.

Jesus expresses this thought in his teaching on singleness (Mt 19:11-12). He speaks of three types of eunuchs, or permanent singles—those who are born without the capacity for normal sexual functioning, those who are made sexually dysfunctional by the cruel action of someone else, and those who purposely choose to stay celibate in order to give their full energies to the work of God's kingdom. He begins his discourse, though, by declaring, "Not everyone can accept this teaching, but only those to whom it has been given," and closes it by saying, "The one who can accept this should accept it." As with Paul, he is saying that the ability joyfully to embrace singleness as a lifetime commitment is a gift of God given to some but not others.

This isn't to say that I can't be chaste and fulfilled as a single person even though I lack the gift of singleness. God will give me all the power needed to stay pure and to enjoy life even though my desire for marriage remains unfulfilled. Yet it will require a measure of discipline and conscious drawing on God's grace which the one with the gift of singleness doesn't have to be concerned with. For that person being single is natural. It requires no heroic discipline.

Paul thus differs from those today who talk of singleness as an ideal to strive for. It must be said, too, that while he speaks highly of the special advantages of being single, he doesn't think of singleness as a higher calling than marriage or as a state in which one is inherently better suited to serve Christ. His enthusiasm for singleness is understandable in light of the fact that this is his gift. But his point in stressing the benefits of singleness is to help those who have this gift be content accepting themselves as a single person and not to feel under any social constraint to marry. It's much the same point that he makes in chapter 12, where he encourages Christians to esteem the gifts they have and not to be envious of one another.

c. A third point about spiritual gifts is that it usually is not difficult to discern what your gifts are. It's striking that nowhere in his lengthy discussion of spiritual gifts in 1 Corinthians 12-14 does Paul offer any guidelines for discovering your gifts. The reason, I'm certain, is because he knew that just as we instinctively recognize that we have hands and feet and other body parts, we naturally discover areas of work which we enjoy and perform competently. As Dr. Ray Stedman notes in *Body Life*, "You discover a spiritual gift just like you discovered your natural talents."[4]

In his excellent book *Your Spiritual Gifts Can Help Your Church Grow*, C. Peter Wagner offers straightforward advice on how to recognize if you have the gift of singleness:

> If you are single and know down in your heart that you would get married in an instant if a reasonable opportunity presented itself, you probably don't have the gift [of singleness]. If you are single and find yourself terribly frustrated by unfulfilled sexual impulses, you probably don't have the gift. But if neither of these things seems to bother you, rejoice—you may have found one of your spiritual gifts.[5]

I heartily concur with Wagner's counsel. Discovering whether God wants you to set your heart on staying single is usually as simple a matter as discerning what it really is you want you to do.

The Bottom Line

What we're saying, then, boils down to several implications:

☐ If you want to be married, you should feel free to stay open to the possibility. You don't have to trouble yourself with thoughts like "What if God really wants me to plan on staying single?" Of course, the final proof that God wants you married will be his making it possible. It would be wrong to think that your desire for marriage is a prophetic indication that God will definitely provide you a mate. Time alone will tell that. But it would be just as wrong to think that he might be expecting you to plan to stay forever single or to take a perpetual vow of celibacy. You are free to stay open and hopeful about the possibility of marriage.

☐ If, on the other hand, you know that you'd prefer to stay single, then you don't have to trouble yourself with the thought "What if God really wants me to be married?" Nor do you have to think of yourself as a second-class citizen of the kingdom of God. You can relax and enjoy the extraordinary gift of singleness God has given you and look for the best ways to invest your life as a single person. And you can tell friends (sensitively, of course) who keep urging you to seek marriage to get off your back.

☐ If you're not certain whether you want to be married or single, don't feel under pressure to have to resolve the issue at this time. Go at your own pace, and let the question sort itself out over time. (My only advice is that you may want to look carefully at whether an underlying fear of commitment is holding you back from doing what you really want to do. The final section of this book deals with that problem, and you may find it helpful to read it through now before going further.)

Is There a Time to Let Go of Your Hope for Marriage?

A remaining question is whether you reach a point with the passing of years or, after a number of failed relationships, where you should conclude that God has shown you through the force of circumstances that he doesn't want you ever to marry. Does the time finally come when you should let go of the desire to marry and set your heart on staying perpetually single?

I want to say emphatically that you never have to conclude that God has told you he never wants you to marry or that he has permanently shut the door unless (a) you decide that you would really prefer to stay single, or (b) he gives you an unusual, supernatural revelation that you should not marry. Apart from either of these occurrences you are not compelled to let go of your hope.

Even a superficial reading of Scripture shows that God has radically different timetables for his children. Some realize important goals early in life, others are late bloomers. This applies as much to the area of finding a mate as to any other.

I was reminded of this recently when a Christian woman friend of mine married for the first time at age fifty. And in *Singles, Sex and Marriage* Herbert J. Miles gives the heartening example and testimony of a woman who was sixty at the time of marriage—his own wife.[6] It was her first marriage, the second for Miles, a widower. I mention these simply as examples; I don't believe there's any upper age limit when you must conclude, "It is now too late for me."

I realize it can be extremely disheartening to move into your later twenties, thirties or perhaps well beyond, wanting to be married but not finding a suitable prospect. I don't mean to minimize the pain involved here at all. Some feel they must give up on their search for marriage and resolve to stay single simply to preserve their mental health. Before you do that, though, let me urge you to read the remainder of this book. It may be that there are changes you can make, either in your perspective on choosing a mate or in the realm of your social life, that will make your search for a spouse more fruitful in the future.

In the meantime don't give up on yourself and remember that Scripture reminds us again and again that prayer and perseverance in our efforts eventually bear fruit. Remember, too, that God is not your adversary but your friend who desires the absolute best for your life. That alone is reason for staying hopeful.

II

God's Guidance
and the
Marriage
Decision

3
Is God a Matchmaker?

A member of the church I attended as a single Christian wrote a song which became a favorite at weddings held there. Many couples began their wedding ceremonies with it, and Evie and I used it as the invocation for our own service as well. The first verse sets forth the theme which continues throughout the song:

Long, long ago, before God gave us life,
Before our souls had substance,
Before our eyes could see,
He planned us for each other,
Each one for the other,
He planned that this day would come to be.[1]

The song proclaims a belief which Christians have long held sacred—that God predetermines whom you marry. If he wants you to be married, there is one ideal choice in his mind for you. And he works in many mysterious ways to bring you to the one for whom you are destined.

Writing this book has challenged me to think back to the decision to include that song, beautiful as it was, in our wedding service and to wonder if it was the wisest and most sensitive choice we could have made. Do I still hold to its premise as strongly as I did then? And was it edifying to proclaim it to others with trumpets as we did in our ceremony?

I have no question that some Christians benefit from the belief that God predestines your spouse. It inspires many married couples to view their relationship as more than a chance occurrence and to appreciate the hand of God in bringing them together. This leads to deeper reverence for Christ and greater faithfulness in their marriage. Many who are single, too, take heart in the thought that if God wants them to be married, he will move mountains to make it happen. They are inspired to stay hopeful and to take the sometimes scary steps needed to find a spouse.

Yet I find just as frequently that this viewpoint has an adverse effect on Christians. Some who are married feel an unhealthy sense of superiority over single friends for having been handpicked by God for the estate of marriage. Others are too quick to blame God for problems that come up in their marriage (see, for example, Gen 3:12!).

Most unfortunate, though, is the paralyzing effect this notion sometimes has on single Christians who want to be married. Some conclude that any personal effort to find a spouse is outside the bounds of faith. Changing jobs or churches to improve the prospects of meeting someone compatible, for instance, is out of the question. Faith demands that you sit still and wait for God to bring the right person to your doorstep.

In one extreme case a Christian woman told me she felt she must avoid any situation that would make it too easy to find a husband. She had four opportunities for missionary service—in three of these, there were single men whom she would consider marrying. Thus she felt compelled to choose the fourth. Though this woman, who was past forty, deeply wanted to be married, she greatly feared getting her own will mixed up with God's in the matter. Making it as difficult as possible for God to bring a man into her life would help ensure that marriage would only come about if God willed.

The belief that God has one ideal choice also leads some to be too idealistic about whom they would consider marrying. Since God is perfect, it is felt that you must not settle for anyone who less than fully measures up to your image of the ideal mate. Such persons are quick to bail out of a relationship at the first sign of another's imperfections, while others wait endlessly for that perfect relationship that never comes along.

Not Going beyond Scripture

I must confess I wince a bit when I remember how Evie and I included the song about God predestining us in our ceremony without considering the effect its message might have on others. I fear, too, that there was something too smug or self-congratulatory in our desire to announce to the world that God had determined from before time to bring us together. I shudder when I think that several other couples who featured this same song in their weddings are now divorced. We certainly tread on delicate ice whenever we declare unreservedly to know particulars of God's hidden plan for our lives.

It's not that I'm ready to reject the premise of the song. My Presbyterian background has given me profound respect for the extensive biblical teaching on God's sovereignty and has taught me to be at home with paradox in the Christian life. I'm comfortable with the thought that God can give us full freedom to choose and act on the human level, yet still on a deeper, more mysterious level be ordering what we do in light of a preconceived plan.

My experience, though, is that most Christians do not find this notion helpful when it comes to decisions related to marriage. In an area as deeply personal, life-changing and far-reaching as moving toward marriage I believe it is vital that we be guided by the most clear and obvious teachings of Scripture and guard against getting side-tracked by speculative notions. Certainly God has told us what he wants us to know clearly and straightforwardly.

Here it is striking that Scripture never specifically states that God predestines a man and woman for each other in marriage. Even though this belief was deeply embedded in Jewish tradition and reflected in a number of sayings and anecdotes in the Talmud, the Holy Spirit did not choose to state matters so specifically in the inspired Scripture. This suggests that, whether or not there is truth in the notion, it is not an edifying one for most believers to keep in mind as they take steps toward marriage. This isn't to say that Scripture has nothing to say about God's role in bringing about marriage. Quite the contrary! But the Bible in general views the responsibility as a *cooperative* one, where both God and we play a part in the process. This is a most liberating concept when it is fully appreciated, but a challenging one as well. To this end Scripture stresses three perspectives which are important to keep in mind.

The Call to Optimism
You have supreme basis for optimism as you seek to find a life partner. While Scripture does not directly address the question of whether God predestines a specific man and woman for each other, it does indicate that he gives a special measure of guidance and help—and very often success—to those who seek the opportunity for marriage.

When Paul, for instance, in 1 Corinthians 7, encourages Christians who need to be married to get married, he shows a remarkable confidence that those seeking a partner will be able to find one. In declaring "let each man have his own wife and each woman her own husband" (v. 2 NEB), he doesn't even entertain the possibility that someone needing marriage will be unable to find an acceptable partner! His optimism is especially intriguing when we remember who he is addressing—a fledgling Christian community barely five years old where the pool of qualified candidates for marriage was surely not vast. Yet Paul's outlook is fueled by faith in a God whose hand is not shortened when it comes to meeting the needs of his saints.

Paul begins his letter to the Corinthians with a declaration of confidence that God will sustain them and meet the deepest needs in their lives:

> I always thank God for you because of his grace given you in Christ Jesus. For in him you have been enriched in every way.... Therefore you do not lack any spiritual gift as you eagerly wait for our Lord Jesus Christ to be revealed. He will keep you strong to the end, so you will be blameless on the day of our Lord Jesus Christ. God, who has called you into fellowship with his Son Jesus Christ our Lord, is faithful. (1 Cor 1:4-8)

This faith in Christ's provision for the Corinthians' needs undergirds all of Paul's remarks in his letter to the young church. He writes with the underlying confidence that as they seek to make intelligent choices, God will work for good in their lives.

To be sure, Paul stops short of guaranteeing that God will provide a spouse to anyone who wants one. Neither here nor anywhere else does Paul, or any biblical writer, lock God into a required response to any human need. There is always the possibility that God will choose not to meet a need directly but to give the grace to live contentedly with unfulfilled desires, a point Paul stresses in his second letter to this church (2 Cor 12:7-10).

Still Paul puts the accent on hope in his teaching on marriage and throughout his writings urges us toward faith in a God who provides all of our needs in Jesus Christ (Phil 4:19). If you want to be married, you certainly have reason to stay hopeful that God will provide someone to meet that need unless he changes your desire or in some clear way shuts the door.

Again, it is important as you maintain this hope to keep your expectations within reasonable bounds. If you're thinking, "God has one ideal choice for me," you may be setting your standards for that person impossibly high. When we consider the perspective on God's role which was in Paul's mind as he wrote 1 Corinthians 7, it seems to be not "God has one ideal person for you to marry," but "God will help you find a *suitable* partner." This is usually a more edifying thought to dwell on. The person whom he gives you to marry will have imperfections and failings, just as you do. Still that person will complement you in a way that will work for your greater happiness and a more fruitful life together for Christ.

The Call to Responsibility

At a party one evening, when this book was in process, I got to talking with a married friend about it. Our conversation wandered onto the question of how faith and personal responsibility work together in finding a spouse. At that moment her husband walked by, and she handed him an empty glass and asked him to fill it with ice for her. I remarked jokingly: "If your faith were strong enough, Molly, your husband would have known you wanted the glass filled without you asking. In fact if your faith were really strong enough, you would have just held the glass out and the ice would have plopped into it!"

She replied: "But isn't this exactly how many Christians are thinking when it comes to finding a partner for marriage? You simply hold the glass out and the ice drops in."

She is right. When we talk about faith, some are left thinking that the burden is completely upon God to bring results. They think that we have no responsibility for the outcome.

Scripture, though, never views matchmaking this way. It always sees it as a mutual process where both God and the one wanting marriage have responsibility for the outcome. It involves not only waiting in faith but taking steps of faith as well.

Thus Paul speaks in 1 Thessalonians 4:4 about the attitude in which a man should "take" a wife, using a verb that implies personal initiative.[2] And in his whole discussion of the importance of marriage in 1 Corinthians 7, he says nothing about waiting passively for God to provide a spouse. Rather, he speaks to individual initiative in saying, "let each man have his own wife and each woman her own husband."

In reality we trust Christ most fully not by sitting idly, but by taking careful, prudent action which we have reason to believe is in line with his will. While there is a certain trust implied by sitting passively and waiting for God to dump the love of your life into your lap, there can be a greater trust involved in taking the often scary steps of changing your circumstances or beginning a new relationship. Such steps are not incompatible with having faith in Christ. When bathed in prayer and a desire to honor him, they are a vital part of what walking in faith involves.

The Call to Accountability

Which brings us to the third perspective which is vital in seeking marriage. Scripture takes the highest possible view of marriage, deeming it a relationship comparable to that of Christ and the church (Eph 5:21-33). To this end I must strive for the highest possible reverence for Christ at each point as I consider the possibility of marriage and take practical steps to bring it about. Thus Paul commands, "For this is the will of God . . . that each of you know how to take a wife for himself in holiness and honor" (1 Thess 4:3-4 RSV).

This speaks to the importance of taking my daily walk with Christ seriously—the need for faithfulness to personal devotions, Bible study, worship, fellowship and support groups. Growing in Christ will not only prepare me to be a better companion to my spouse, but will enhance the Lord's freedom to work out his best in my life, for marriage and all areas. Part of this growth process is praying regularly about my hopes for marriage. I should give attention both to asking

God for grace to do his will and to expressing honestly what my desires are at the present time. Finally, this passage speaks to the need to make the most responsible, sanctified decisions I can as I take steps to find a relationship and, ultimately, decide about whether to marry a particular person. At each point my goal should be to understand and do God's will.

While knowing that God wants me to seek a relationship with him presents a challenge, it brings me back to a basis for hope as well, for it reminds me that he wants to work for good at all points in my life. He is not my adversary but my friend, one who desires the very best for my future. As the psalmist declares: "He redeems my life from the pit and crowns me with love and compassion. He satisfies my desires with good things, so that my youth is renewed like the eagle's" (Ps 103:4-5). That is incentive enough to seek to honor Christ in every way as I take steps toward marriage!

4
How Can I
Know
God's Will?

I must admit that I decided to ask Evie to marry me without receiving any direct revelation to do it. I deeply wanted God's will and, in fact, made my choice during a day set aside for prayer and meditation. But I approached the decision more rationally than mystically. I weighed the pros and cons. In the end I decided to propose to her mainly because it seemed to make the most sense to do so.

If this sounds like a bit of true confessions, it's not because I'm doubting now that I made the right choice (far from it!). Yet I now realize that as a young believer, I wasn't always at home with such a practical approach to decision making. There were many people telling me how to know God's will during that time, most of them saying that I should wait for God to show me in a dramatic and clear-cut way what to do.

Gradually, as I became more acquainted with Scripture, I began to see it presenting a rather different—and, frankly, more liberating—picture of guidance. While the early Christians were strongly confident God was leading them, there is little evidence that they frequently received dramatic guidance from God. They tended to make their decisions in a logical manner, even taking major steps of faith without any supernatural leading. By the time I decided to marry Evie, I had grown fairly comfortable with taking a practical approach to major decisions. Still, I went back and forth on the question.

Since that time I've studied Scripture intently on the matter, and my first book was devoted to the topic of guidance. I can now say confidently that this *is* the approach to guidance that is recommended in the Bible. God is pictured as one who guides through our rational decision process, not apart from it. There is abundant evidence that guidance, as one writer has put it, usually boils down to sanctified thinking.

I find that Christian singles today, though, are more typically at the point where I was as a young believer—not fully comfortable with this idea. Many feel guilty even thinking of the marriage decision as a "choice."

"Shouldn't you wait for God to impress his will on you in some unmistakable manner?" they ask. "Isn't it wrong to make much effort to think things through?"

Voices preaching such notions about God's will continue to prevail throughout our Christian culture. There are three perspectives on guidance that are especially common which discourage practical thinking and often cause confusion for those who are considering marriage.

With the Heart or with the Mind?
One is that a decision for marriage should be approached intuitively

rather than rationally—more with the heart than with the mind. While this is not a uniquely Christian concept, it is often adopted in a particularly Christian way to explain how we receive God's guidance.

I first heard this belief proclaimed by a pastor whom I greatly respected, in a talk which he gave on the first retreat I attended as a new Christian. He said: "When you've met the person God wants you to marry, you'll know instinctively that this is the one. You won't be able to explain your choice. Yet you'll have no doubt at all that it's God's will. If anyone asks you how you know, all you can say is 'I know in my heart that this is the right person.' If you can give a reason for your choice, then it's not God's leading."

I remember with amusement how later in the same retreat another pastor from the same church, whom I also highly esteemed, addressed the same issue in a talk which he gave. Not having heard the first pastor's talk, he declared: "It is vital to use your mind in selecting a marriage partner. You need to have good reasons for your choice. Beware of making this choice without carefully thinking it through." To say the least, as a new Christian I was thoroughly confused!

I must say in deference to both of these men that they each have had excellent marriages. I have no question that they each made a good choice, one through an intuitive approach, one through a more rational one. It suggests that God undoubtedly creates some of us to be more intuitive by nature and some more cognitive.

Yet I have also known many Christians who entered marriage with great conviction of heart, knowing for certain that God was leading them, whose marriages have not endured nearly as well. About half of the ones I'm thinking of have ended in divorce. In many cases it now seems only too plain that the decision to marry was based too much on an inner impression and that not enough time was taken to assess whether the broad sort of compatibility needed for a marriage commitment was really there.

I've known so many, too, who thought that they had an inner leading to marry someone who never came to share their conviction.

If I confess another's sin here, I must confess my own also. One afternoon as a young Christian I was praying in a pleasant mountain park setting when my thoughts wondered to a young woman in the college fellowship, whom I knew only casually. As one thought led to another, I mused over what it would feel like to be married to her. The feeling was good. I concluded that God was giving me a vision that we would someday marry.

I had the audacity (though of course I didn't think of it as such at the time) to go and share my "vision" with this woman, only to be told that God had not spoken to her in any such way. In fact, she made it clear that she had no interest whatever in a romantic relationship with me.

Yet for some time after that I continued to cherish the conviction that she would someday come to her senses and see God's will as I did. Neither friends nor pastors could convince me of the folly of my thoughts. I knew that God had spoken to me, and that was that.

I could fill this book with stories of Christians who've shared similar experiences with me. Many men and not a few woman have told me of receiving a vision to marry someone which was never reciprocated. And I've counseled with so many, especially women, who have been at their wit's end in knowing how to deal with a presumptuous friend who is laying such a mandate on them.

I've seen time and again the unfortunate delusions that can come from thinking that one's instinct is the unfailing voice of God. Sadly, I've also been close to some relationships which would have made excellent marriages, yet one or the other was waiting for a degree of inner conviction that was not reasonable to expect.

Why, then, does the intuitive approach, which seems to work so well for some, present so many problems for others? Here it's important to understand what the experience of intuition actually is. When we experience a strong inner conviction, a sudden flash of insight or sense of inner leading such as I had on the mountain, the experience should be understood not primarily as a spiritual but a *psychological* one. Our mistake comes in thinking that intuition is the direct voice of the Holy Spirit and thus a call to action which is permanently laid upon us. In reality intuition is a glimpse into our subconscious mind. It tells us what underneath we are really thinking and feeling.[1]

Thus intuition is very important, for our subconscious mind often does a much better job of processing information than our conscious mind does. Yet in the end, our intuition is only as good as the information which has gone into it. A sudden flash that God wants me to marry a certain person is invariably influenced by all the ideas I've ever been exposed to about the ideal mate. Yet new information and new understanding may lead to a new sense of intuition.

From this standpoint, I always have the right to question my intuition. I'm never bound to follow its mandate, and I never have the right to try to lock someone else into its dictate. When in a serious relationship I've really taken the time to get to know the other person, and we've explored the possibility of marriage in sensible ways, then I can begin to trust what my intuition tells me. Yet often the conviction that comes at this point is quite different from impressions I had at the beginning of the relationship. In one important survey of over a thousand happily married people, eighty per cent "reported they did not feel an immediate attraction to each other when they first met."[2]

This is not to suggest that my inner impression must be unwavering before I can go ahead with marriage. Many of us are so constituted psychologically that such unerring certainty is not possible. This is a point I want to return to in a moment. Here let it simply be said that the marriage decision should be made as much with the head as with the heart. God has commanded that we love him with all our mind as well as with all of our hearts, and it's vital that we apply the mind he's given us to the most important choice many of us are ever privileged to make.

Do I Need a Special Sign?
While some Christians place too much weight on intuition, others

assume that a special sign is needed from God about whom to marry. The problems that result from this assumption are similar to those that come from spiritualizing intuition.

Some couples who have good reason to consider marriage hold back in the belief that they need a special indication from God to go ahead. One couple whom I counseled, Rick and Sandy, who had dated for over two years, told me that they had asked God to give them a sign by a certain date to continue their relationship. Otherwise they would break up. When I asked them what specific sign they expected, they said that they didn't know. They simply wanted God to show them in some unmistakable way what to do.

Rick and Sandy illustrate the irony that is common to many who look for a special sign from God—the fact that often there is no clear idea what precisely that sign should be. This ambiguity leaves many Ricks and Sandys waiting indefinitely for marching orders.

It leaves others open to seeing signs that are really not there. A couple in the first church I attended met initially on a vacation trip to Europe. Later they encountered each other unexpectedly in a church in the U.S. They took this extraordinary coincidence as a sign from God that they should marry. Tragically, their marriage lasted only six months. They simply had not done their homework in getting to know each other and in thinking through whether they were compatible. They were too quick to read supernatural guidance into an unusual circumstance.

To be sure, some Christians do specify to God what sign they want, a practice often called "putting out a fleece," in reference to Gideon's experience in Judges 6. One notable Christian described how he sought God's will about whether to marry his girlfriend: He mailed letters to two different friends, praying that God would show his will by the timing of the replies, but not telling his friends what was on his mind. If replies came back on the same day, he'd assume God wanted them to marry; if they came on different days, this would mean God's answer was no. When return letters from both friends

arrived in the same delivery, he concluded that God spoken affirm-
atively and went ahead and proposed marriage.

I don't deny that God may on occasion honor such a fleece offered
in innocence by a sincere Christian. Yet there is no biblical promise
that he's bound to do so. To the contrary, there's no example in the
New Testament after Pentecost of believers seeking God's will through
a fleece; the last instance was the disciples casting lots for Judas's
successor (Acts 1:15-26), which occurred before the Holy Spirit was
given on Pentecost. This indicates, I believe, that the Spirit-filled believer has all the inner resources needed for wise decision making.
Fleecing is generally a diversion from taking proper responsibility for
our decisions.

It's interesting, too, that on those exceptional occasions after Pentecost when extraordinary supernatural guidance was given, it was
always to instruct the disciples to do something which they wouldn't
have chosen on the basis of reason alone. Philip's guidance by the
angel to leave the dramatic revival in Samaria and go off to a desert
road is a good example (Acts 8:26-40). In the great majority of personal decisions noted in the New Testament, God's will was determined simply through a logical decision, apart from any unusual
guidance. For what it's worth, apart from Joseph's revelation from the
angel to marry Mary, there is no instance in the New Testament of
anyone basing a marriage decision on supernatural guidance. Nor is
there any statement suggesting that a special sign should be sought
in a marriage decision.

My advice to couples who are looking for a sign from God about
whether to marry is that God will give them a sign—the evidence that
they are compatible for marriage discovered in the normal process of
building a relationship. It will be found not through some unusual or
supernatural indication but through getting to know each other and
using the gift of judgment which God has given them to make wise
decisions. We must remember that Scripture promises that we who
follow Christ have the mind of Christ (1 Cor 2:16). This mind, as Paul

understands it, is not a passive one which waits for information to be dumped into it but a mind that *thinks*. It's no less than the capacity to make wise judgment.

The question that's often raised at this point is, what then is the meaning of Proverbs 3:5, which commands us, "Trust in the Lord with all your heart, and do not rely on your own insight" (RSV). Doesn't this imply that we lack the ability to make good decisions? It must be remembered, though, that Proverbs not only gives us this command but numerous others which enjoin us to exercise wisdom and make sound decisions. By telling us not to rely on our own insights, the verse cautions us against trying to resolve our decisions without trusting in the guidance and provision of God. The point isn't that we shouldn't strive to make good decisions. To the contrary, when we've put our trust in Christ and earnestly sought his direction, we have basis for an uncanny trust that he is guiding our decision process.

Should Someone Else Make the Decision for Me?

While some Christians look for direct guidance through inner impressions or special signs, others put great weight on the need for someone else to tell them God's will. A popular seminar has taught that parents, whether Christian or not, have chain-of-command authority to decree God's will for the marriage choice of their children. While I don't find Christians as fast to accept this premise anymore, many still hold it as gospel.

Much more common today is a philosophy of spiritual leadership which holds that pastors or church elders have the authority to decide whom those under their care should marry. A surprising number of churches, including some large dynamic ones, follow this ideology. It is occasionally embraced by certain parachurch ministries as well.

Still other Christians believe that someone with a special gift of prophecy may be able to tell you whom God wants you to marry, even though that person may have no relation to you or be in any special position of spiritual authority—or for that matter have had any previous acquaintance with you at all. Some of the most tragic examples I've seen of one person claiming to know God's will for whom someone else should marry have involved those claiming to have a gift of prophecy.

In one case a high school student who was far from ready for a lifetime commitment married because a strong-minded adult in his church prophesied that he should do so. In another a college freshman, Elizabeth, was told by an older woman in her church that God wanted her to marry Ken, a man in the church whom she scarcely knew. As an impressionable new Christian, Elizabeth assumed that this older woman, who spoke with such authority, had a handle on God's will which she lacked. She opened herself to a friendship with Ken; in time a dating relationship developed, and Ken proposed marriage. By now Elizabeth was in love with him and she accepted. Shortly afterward Ken broke the engagement and within one month married someone else.

When I met Elizabeth on an InterVarsity retreat, she was a college senior and had only recently overcome two years of severe depression over the incident. Not only was there the pain of rejection, difficult enough for most to endure, but great confusion about the meaning of the prophecy. Was it Elizabeth's fault that it failed? Ken's? Or was the woman who prophesied misguided in the first place?

It's experiences like this which remind me how extremely important it is for each of us to have a clear understanding of biblical teaching on the role of others in personal guidance. Scripture does stress that counsel is crucial in our decision making. A number of times the Proverbs declare, "In a *multitude* of counselors there is strength." Thus wisdom comes from many counselors, not from the dogmatic view of a single individual. With a multitude of counselors will likely come a multitude of opinions. Through them, my mind is stretched to think more deeply and farsightedly about my decision. Even if what I end up doing differs from what anyone has advised me, I've still benefited greatly from the whole counseling process. I must take responsibility for my own decisions, calling the shots as best as I can. Never does Scripture teach that I must follow the dictate of any one individual.

But what about the claims of those who insist otherwise? The verse that is usually quoted to show that our parents' opinion must prevail in a marriage decision is Colossians 3:20: "Children, obey your parents in everything, for this pleases the Lord." Yet the Greek word for children *(ta tekna)* denotes a young child, not an adult son or daughter. The command simply does not, as is claimed, lay a mandate on grown children to continue to follow their parents' dictates. While the injunction to honor our parents is always with us, we're not held to a rigid chain-of-command adherence to their directives.

The same point applies to the authority of spiritual leaders. There's no indication that those in leadership positions in the New Testament had the prerogative to direct the personal decisions of those under them. Spiritual leaders were deemed great authority to direct the affairs of the church and to declare the doctrinal and moral will of God. But that authority didn't extend to the personal choices of parishioners, such as where to work or whom to marry.[3]

Neither does the New Testament teach that the gift of prophecy enables one person to know God's will for the personal decisions of someone else. Charismatic writer Michael Harper, who writes with great esteem for the gift of prophecy, notes that "guidance" is not one of its functions:

Prophecies which tell other people what they are to do—are to be regarded with great suspicion. "Guidance" is never indicated as one of the uses of prophecy. For instance, although Cornelius was told by an angel to send for Peter (Acts 10:5), Peter himself was told to go with them through an independent agency (Acts 10:20). There may be exceptions to this—but if so they are very rare. This gift is not intended to take the place of common sense or the wisdom which comes from God and which manifests itself through our natural faculties.[4]

I'm comfortable telling Christians that while they should graciously receive the counsel which others give them, they should be thick-skinned (though not discourteous) with those who insist beyond a reasonable point that they know God's will for them. I'm not helping others by letting them think they can play Christ in my life. God has not created any person to be able to handle such a role. And I'm not helping myself by letting someone else make a decision for me which God wants me to take responsibility for resolving. Knowing God's will for my life is *my* responsibility. Others can help. But they cannot replace the need for careful thinking and evaluation on my part.

5
Can I
Be
Certain?

▲▲▲▲▲

R ecently a twenty-four-year-old woman, Rita, phoned me, anxious for my advice. She had been through two dating relationships in which her hopes were seriously disappointed. Finally, she had taken a step to keep the pattern from repeating. She told the Lord that she wouldn't date another man unless her mom was confident that he was the one she should marry. She was bound and determined not to make a mistake about God's will again.

After making her resolution, Tom asked Rita out. Her mom felt that Tom would make an excellent husband for her, so Rita accepted, eagerly hoping she'd finally found the Lord's choice. The time with Tom was enjoyable and only intensified her hope. Yet unfortunately six months had now passed and she hadn't heard from him again.

Rita not only felt rejected but terribly confused about what all of this meant about God's will. How could her mother have been so confident and Tom not be following through? Should she simply assume that Tom was God's choice and continue to wait?

I told Rita that I admired her respect for her mother's opinion. Our parents' counsel is so important in our big decisions. Yet, to expect her mom to know the mind of God unerringly in this matter was to lay a burden on her too great for any human to bear. Rita would ultimately need to make her own decision, weighing her mom's advice along with other factors.

Rita didn't dispute what I said, but in frustration replied, "How, then, can I know *for certain?*" In other words, if her mom's advice were not an infallible sign of God's will, what would be?

Here we came to the heart of her dilemma. Rita assumed that she could have certainty about God's will for her marriage choice apart from discovering it in the step-by-step process of building a relationship. Rather than seeing God's will as something to be discerned through her experience, she assumed it could be found in some external way beforehand.

Rita's assumption brings us to the heart of the problem behind the desire of most people for direct guidance. Underlying the desire for guidance through inner impressions, special signs or someone else's pronouncement, is usually the belief that perfect certainty about God's will is attainable. While many would not go as far as Rita in thinking that certainty can be realized before a relationship begins, many— probably most—Christians assume that absolute certainty is needed before a decision to marry someone can be made.

An Understandable Desire

The desire for perfect certainty is only too easy to understand. We don't like making even minor commitments without the assurance that we've exhausted our options. Yet we may decide to join a church, declare a college major, take a job, even buy a home in less than full confidence that our choice is the best possible one, knowing that our commitment doesn't lock us in forever. Change can always be made, and at least we'll learn from our experiences. The marriage decision offers no such freedom. For Christians, who take the inviolability of marriage vows with steely seriousness, marriage is a no-turning-back proposition. As a twenty-seven-year-old friend of mine, whose decision to marry his girlfriend has been on again/off again, expressed it, "I expect to be married to her for fifty years. That's a long time to live with the wrong decision."

Our desire for perfect certainty in the marriage decision is also fueled by many fantasies and idealized pictures which we carry of the romantic relationship. Since childhood we've seen it, again and again, through literature and the media: man meets woman and both instantly recognize that they've found their one true love. As a result, it's deeply ingrained in our minds that when two people are destined for one another, they know with a certainty that is immediate and absolute.

Yet our Christian teaching has often done just as much to encourage such a notion. We've heard so many stories of those who knew that they knew that they knew, and we've heard it said so many times that when you've met God's choice there will be no doubting at all. Our evangelical tradition, too, with its great and proper emphasis upon the sovereignty of God, leaves us assuming that a God who is all-powerful wouldn't possibly leave us with less than perfect certainty that we've found the one of his choice. To assume anything less would be irreverent, an insult to the greatness of God and his ability to guide his children.

Faith and Feelings

Here, though, we must be clear about where certainty is promised by Scripture and where it isn't. Scripture declares that we who are born again of Christ have basis for immense confidence in him. We can have certainty of his intention to grant us eternal life, as well as of his determination to guide us in the very best paths between now and when we go to be with him. John 10 attests that Christ takes the same sort of autocratic but benevolent authority in our lives which a good shepherd takes for his sheep. Through many beautiful, poetic statements John presents Christ as one who not only has our very best in mind but has both the power and determination to lead us into it.

> When he has brought out all his own, he goes on ahead of them, and his sheep follow him because they know his voice. But they will never follow a stranger; in fact, they will run away from him because they do not recognize a stranger's voice (vv. 4-5).

> I am the gate; whoever enters through me will be saved. He will come in and go out, and find pasture. The thief comes only to steal and kill and destroy; I have come that they may have life, and have it to the full (vv. 9-10).

> My sheep listen to my voice; I know them, and they follow me. I give them eternal life, and they shall never perish; no one can snatch them out of my hand (vv. 27-28).

The implication of the biblical promise of guidance is that when I desire God's will and am prayerfully seeking it, I may have confidence that he is guiding my whole decision-making process. This means that the decisions I end up making are the ones he wants me to make. Clearly this promise extends to the most far-reaching decision most of us ever have to make as Christians: the decision about whether or not to marry.

Yet never does Scripture promise that we will necessarily *feel* certain, to the point of no hint of doubt, in the decisions we make. It's here that we must remember the timeless distinction between faith and feelings. Faith is "the conviction of things not seen" (Heb 11:1 RSV). In other words, it's the belief that something is true even though we have less than complete evidence to support our conviction. It's the decision to believe something even though some room for doubt remains. Where perfect certainty exists, there is no need for faith!

Substantial Certainty

This is not to say that faith is an unthinking or foolhardy attitude. We commit ourselves to trust in Christ's salvation, to yield our lives into his hands and to believe in the infallibility of Scripture, on the basis of substantial evidence that God exists, that he has revealed himself through Christ, that Christ rose from the dead and that the Scriptures have been divinely inspired by him. Yet we would be hard put to offer absolute proof for any of these claims. We have chosen to make a leap of faith on the basis of reasonable evidence, even very reasonable evidence, but not proof. Proof would remove the need for faith.

It's in this same spirit that the decision for marriage is to be made. Generous time should be allowed for getting to know the other person, and keen attention should be given to all the compatibility factors that could make for a healthy union or a difficult one. Yet for most of us the point comes where a leap of faith is needed. We will need to go ahead and commit ourselves in the face of something less than uncompromising certainty.

Charlie W. Shedd, from his decades of experience in family counseling, addresses the issue of certainty in choosing a mate in *How to Know If You're Really in Love—Really in Love Enough for Marriage*. He relates a letter a young woman sent him and then his response:

Dear Dr. Shedd:
Terry and I have been going together for over a year now and he keeps asking me to marry him. He really is great in so many ways, and I don't know what's the matter, but somehow I can't make up my mind. Is there any way a girl can be one hundred percent sure so that she never ever doubts? Please can you help me decide?

[Response:]
Wish I could, but should anyone ever try to be one hundred percent sure? I doubt it. Those who say they are absolutely certain, with never a look back, may have turned their brains off. They

could be living on emotion, minus intellect. So the goal is to begin at fifty-one percent surety, then build that to seventy-five, eight-five, ninety.[1]

I like the way Dr. Shedd puts it. As we move ahead, our sense of certainty can increase. Yet for most of us, the ninety-per-cent level is probably about it. Most of us are so constituted that perfect certainty about anything is simply not a realistic goal. Those of us who are deep thinkers too quickly see possible exceptions to our conclusions. In the marriage decision we realize that we've met only a minute number of those of the opposite sex, and our acquaintance time with the one we're considering marrying has been extremely brief compared to the span of time we expect to be married. It's simply not reasonable to think that we could muster such a heroic degree of certainty that all measure of doubt is gone.

Deciding to Decide

Those of us who by nature are more feeling-oriented may indeed feel strongly assured at a given time that we have found the one for whom we were destined. Yet given new discoveries about our loved one or about ourselves, given new circumstances, given indigestion or a poor night's sleep, our feelings may change. If we simply look at how convictions in other matters have wavered in the past, we must conclude that we can't bank on the intensity of our present conviction continuing forever.

Yet we can take control of our lives. We can conclude that in spite of lingering uncertainties or mood swings, we do have substantial evidence that we and another would make good life partners and that we are both at a point of maturity where it makes sense to go ahead with marriage. This is the very good news side of what we're saying— it's O.K. to go ahead even with a commitment as momentous as marriage with less than perfect certainty. Indeed, it's not only O.K. but *necessary* for most of us to do so if we want to do the kind of inertia-breaking that will be needed to forge a marriage commitment.

I realize that some will claim that the perspective I'm recommending is something less than the victorious life in the Spirit which the New Testament proclaims. I would contend just the opposite. It is indeed in those situations where we have the opportunity to go ahead with a decision in the face of substantial but less than perfect certainty that the greatest opportunities for walking in faith occur. By choosing to marry someone on this basis, I'm thrusting myself into the hands of Christ, trusting that he is too big to let me make a mistake—or that if I have, he'll find a way to redirect me.

It's among those who are banking on perfect certainty that we often observe the least victorious spirit. Many who are in solid relationships which would make excellent marriages are waiting endlessly for a level of certainty that is simply not reasonable to expect. Others, like Rita, are locked into unhealthy situations because they believe God has given them a sign that they must stay there.

Some of the most tragic situations I've seen involve those with highly sanguine personalities, who are subject to strong mood swings, who go back and forth in their conviction to marry. One such woman whom I've counseled with has called her engagement on and off about a half-dozen times. Though she is a deeply intelligent woman in her young thirties, holding a challenging job in the medical profession, she's letting an unreasonable ideal of certainty control her decision about marriage, rather than her own good judgment.

Confronting Your Ambivalence

Those of us who find ourselves over a long period of time going through extreme emotional swings which make commitment difficult, may profit from professional help. Underlying these mood swings may be a fear of commitment itself. With a skilled counselor we can explore factors in our background that contribute to this fear. We may likely discover that our childhood experience of love was inconsistent, leaving us gun-shy about trusting ourselves to anyone who professes too strongly to love us now. While such discoveries are painful, it is far easier in the long run to deal with reality than with emotional surges which we don't understand. With the right help we can come to terms with our past in a way that puts us in a better position to make confident choices in the present.

Yet we may also have to come to terms with our view of God's guidance. If we are cherishing the assumption that we can achieve perfect certainty before undertaking major steps, that assumption will need to be revised. The Christian life is not a fantasy experience where our life moves are constantly revealed in neon lights or through unswerving mystical impressions, leaving us with no need to think or wrestle things through.

To the contrary, Scripture portrays the Christian experience as an adventure of faith, where we never know what is around the bend, but inch ahead a step at time. We always have just enough light to take the next step, yet need to take that step in order to see clearly enough to take the step beyond. While we have great confidence in the one who guides us and protects us, we are constantly put in the position where from the human standpoint we must take steps that seem to be risks. Yet it is precisely such steps that incline us most fully to trust in Christ, who alone knows the future and who alone can continue to give us the light unto our path. Through the whole experience comes a sense of life that, while often challenging, is never boring.

The marriage decision is in no way exempt from this adventure of faith. Indeed, it is often the greatest opportunity this life affords to experience what walking in faith is all about.

III
Choosing
a
Spouse

6

Do You Feel
Deep Compassion
for the
Other Person?

Y ou're a wonderful woman, Jamie. In fact, remarkable. Whoever marries you will be extremely fortunate. But I'm not that man. I just don't believe it's right for us to marry."

Harold rehearsed his lines over and over, steeling himself for the dreaded announcement he felt he must make. He would rather let his relationship with Jamie linger on indefinitely. Yet he knew that it wasn't fair to keep her tied up in a romance that might go nowhere. He owed her a clear answer so that she could get on with her life.

Harold (twenty-five) and Jamie (twenty-six) had talked long and often about marriage during more than two years of dating. But while Jamie had been convinced about marriage for some time, Harold remained confused, not certain that his affection for her had the intensity of marriage love.

Harold knew that he cared deeply for Jamie, and their friendship had been a source of great strength and encouragement to him. He had been, in fact, no less than astonished by their broad compatibility and many areas of common interest. Though physical attraction had been minimal on his part at first, it had developed in time and seemed to be growing.

Yet Harold knew that he was capable of stronger physical and romantic feelings than Jamie aroused in him. Several women had done more to turn his head in the past. In several other ways, too, Jamie fell short of his ideal. She was less athletic and generally less ambitious than Harold assumed his wife should be. Thus, Harold had concluded that the evidence for them marrying just wasn't strong enough. The only reasonable step was to level with Jamie and break things off.

As he came close to telling Jamie though, he was filled with remorse at the thought of disappointing her. He realized, too, how much he wanted to make her happy. The thought of bringing her joy through marriage brought him immense pleasure as he mused on it. It was almost startling to face this.

He was struck, too, with how much he wanted her to succeed. It was exciting to imagine her finishing her master's degree and finding the research position she had long dreamed of. He enjoyed thinking about how their supportive relationship could enhance her success.

Wisely, before making a final decision, Harold decided to seek counsel from an insightful pastor friend who knew both him and Jamie well. After sharing for nearly an hour about the relationship and his confusion about marriage, Harold concluded by saying: "Pastor Bill, I really want what is best for Jamie. I long for her to be happy. Yet I think it would be wrong to marry mainly from sympathy."

Pastor Bill quickly replied, "I agree with you, Harold. Marriages based on sympathy are bound for disaster. Yet the feelings for Jamie that you described to me are not sympathy but compassion. Marriages based on compassion are bound to prosper."

"What is the difference?" Harold asked.

"Sympathy is merely feeling sorry for someone," Pastor Bill replied. "Compassion is more positive and dynamic. You desire the other to be happy, to prosper, to experience God's very best."

Then after a long pause, Pastor Bill said gently but firmly: "I've got news for you, Harold. You're in love with this woman. You'd be crazy to let this one get away."

Identifying the Feeling

It may seem strange to suggest that someone would have to be told that he or she is in love. This flies in the face of the popular notion that when true love strikes, the sensation is so overwhelming that you have about as much chance of missing it as you would a rhinoceros in a wading pool. Yet cases like Harold's are common. There's a subtle nature to marriage-quality love which can easily escape our notice. This is especially true when we've been programmed, as Harold was, with ideas that hit wide of the mark of what marriage love is all about.

Many, like Harold, have so set their expectations that they are slow to identify healthy love when they actually experience it. Others fall into the pattern of thinking that suggests a passionate attraction will provide the basis for a sound marriage.

What, then, is the essence of marriage-quality love? Pastor Bill was right. Compassion is the basis of this love. Romantic love then mixes compassion together with friendship and sexual attraction.

There are many feelings which can attract and bond you to someone else. When love is truly from God, foremost among these is compassion. You feel the other's hurts and concerns as your own. You ache to see God's best worked out in that person's life.

The dazed sensation which we call "being in love" often has little to do with compassion. It can come from sexual attraction alone or from being enamored with qualities you esteem in the other. It can come when the other makes up for a deficit in your own life. It can come from the wonderful gratification of knowing that someone else cherishes you exactly as you are.

Pastor Jim Conway says it simply: Someone "may say, 'I'm in love with you,' but what he really means is, 'You meet my needs and make me happy.' "[1]

Don't get me wrong. When God gives you love of marriage quality for another person, you'll have great hope that the other will meet your needs. This is an important part of the emotional mix that melds you to another person's life. Paul says clearly in 1 Corinthians 7 that unless you need the benefits of marital companionship, stay single.

Yet when love has been brewed in your heart by God, you're possessed with a deep and often surprising desire to meet the other person's needs as well. Early on in my relationship with Evie I began to realize that I felt compassion for her in a stronger way than had been present in other dating relationships. This was a crucial factor in concluding that God was prompting us to get married. And compassion has been an important motivating factor in our sixteen years of happy marriage. As a basically selfish person, such selfless love does not come easily to me and can only be supernatural.

Assessing Your Compassion

If you are in a serious relationship and considering marriage, let me suggest a test. Imagine something unfortunate happening to the person you're thinking of marrying. Picture him or her being rejected or fired from a cherished job opportunity, failing a program in school or having some experience which would be a blow to his or her self-esteem. Does the thought of this happening fill you with sorrow? Or does it, rather, bring you a certain gratification and relief?

When your affection for another person is based mainly on what they can do for you, you may actually rejoice inwardly at their setbacks (though feigning sorrow on the outside), for you perceive that their misfortune will make them more dependent upon you. At the same time you feel intimidated by their accomplishments. And you may feel terribly uneasy over them having strong friendships outside of your relationship.

When compassion is strong, you find yourself naturally desiring what is best for the other person. You're not threatened by the thought of his or her success—indeed, you rejoice in it. The requirements of 1 Corinthians 13 and Ephesians 5:21-33 don't seem like duties but as guidelines that are natural to fulfill. Not that there won't be times when you feel jealous or fearful of losing the other's affection. None of us is perfect, and humanness invades every relationship. But overall, you are comfortable with the other person developing her gifts, having successful experiences and even special friendships outside of your own. And when the other suffers a disappointment, you feel it with him.

Compassion in Scripture

Though Scripture gives few examples of couples in the courtship or engagement stages, there are two which provide striking pictures of compassion. We see a magnificent demonstration of compassion in the way Joseph, the father of Jesus, treated Mary. Though we're told little about this intriguing man, what we are told shows that he had an exemplary love for his wife-to-be.

When Joseph discovered that Mary was pregnant, it is said that he resolved to break off the relationship quietly (Mt 1:19). At this point Joseph didn't know that Mary's pregnancy was of supernatural origin but assumed she had been promiscuous. What's amazing is that Joseph didn't make a public display of Mary's unfaithfulness. He had every right to do so, in fact would have been expected to in order to save face for himself. But he resolved to break the engagement in a way that would be least humiliating to her. He showed great compassion for her even in the midst of this apparent transgression.

There's little question in my mind that this gracious spirit in Joseph was an important reason why God trusted him with the gift of marriage to Mary and the privilege of being father of our Lord.

Another impressive example of compassion is Boaz's treatment of

Ruth in the book of Ruth (Ruth 3—4). Boaz awakes at midnight to find Ruth sitting at the end of his bed. Though he could easily have taken advantage of her in this vulnerable and enticing situation, he resisted all inclination to do so. And though his subsequent decision to marry her suggests that he greatly wanted her for his wife, he first allowed a closer kin the opportunity to exercise his right to marry her. He showed kindness and fairness at every point.

It is of considerable interest to me that both Joseph and Boaz were willing to accept even the ending of a relationship, as painful as that option might be. This is always the response of compassionate persons, when they know it's in the best interest of the other. It's in the unhealthy, addictive relationship that one feels that he or she must hold on (no matter what the cost) to the other.

This is an important point, for sometimes one takes the fact that he or she is willing to terminate a relationship as indication that their love is not sufficiently strong for marriage. Ironically, the very willingness to let the relationship go may indicate that compassion is strong enough to recommend marriage. This was part of what convinced Pastor Bill about Harold's love for Jamie. And it has been part of what has persuaded me on several occasions to encourage someone to take a second look at a relationship they were thinking of abandoning.

I don't, of course, mean to suggest that the willingness to end a relationship always suggests that true marriage-love is present. Many times it does not. Yet sometimes it shows in a paradoxical way that love runs deeper than one realizes.

Sorting It Through

If you find yourself, like Harold, confused about how to interpret your feelings for someone whom you're dating, and especially if it has been a long-term relationship, I would strongly recommend finding a qualified person with whom you can talk things through. A trusted Christian friend in an enduring, healthy marriage is a good bet. Or a pastor. I personally count it one of my greatest privileges to be able to help someone in this area. I know most pastors feel the same. You needn't be hesitant about approaching your pastor on this matter.

If you realize that you don't feel true compassion for the person you're thinking of marrying, this means two possible things. Either God is not calling you to marry this person, or else you need to allow more time for compassion to grow. In any case, it wouldn't be right to think of marriage to this person at this time. I realize my words may seem cold and academic, while it may be indescribably difficult to think of not going through with marriage if your heart has been strongly set on it. Yet I must tell you honestly that whatever pain is involved in changing your plans will be mercifully less than the pain experienced in an unsatisfactory marriage.

Without compassion as the foundation of your love for this person, you'll set yourself up for much disappointment and rob yourself of the opportunity to experience the deepest joys which marriage affords. Your happiness will rise or fall on how well you feel the other is meeting your needs. You'll probably experience a lot of ongoing stress from worrying about factors that might detract the other from being fully attentive to you. You'll miss the deep pleasure that comes from sharing empathetically in the successes and victories of your spouse and the bonding of spirit that comes from sharing sorrows. Over time your expectations will make it more and more difficult for the other, no matter how benevolent he or she is, to fulfill your needs.

You will, in short, do yourself an unbelievable favor by deciding not to go through with marriage to this person. Trust God that when the time is right and the person is right, you'll feel the kind of compassion we're talking about. Ask him to do whatever is necessary to stretch your heart and to make it possible for you to experience this kind of love for someone of the opposite sex.

On the other hand, if compassion for your prospective partner is strong, realize that you have the single most important indication that your love is from God and is of the quality that could make for a healthy marriage. As undramatic as your feelings for this person may seem to be, you may be experiencing the seeds of a dynamic marriage-quality love. Even though you don't feel dazed, crazed or moonstruck over this person, if you truly *care* for him or her, you have the most essential ingredient for a vibrant marriage.

A Two-Way Street

I must add that it's just as important that the other feels compassion for you. It might seem that the most self-sacrificing, Christian thing to do is to go ahead and marry someone for whom you feel deep compassion, even though it's not reciprocated. As noble as the idea might sound, though, I can assure you that (and relieve you because) this isn't in God's will for you.

God's ideal for marriage is one in which two people share both compassion and personal fulfillment. Though we can argue that it should be otherwise, in reality your ability to give of yourself in marriage is at least partly dependent upon the fulfillment you receive from your spouse. This is how God has created us as humans, and we cannot escape the fact. There is give and take in every healthy marriage; if it's all give on your part and no receiving, eventually your steam will run out. You don't have what it takes to be a savior to someone in marriage, and God isn't calling you to take on that role.

Realize, too, that you'll not be helping the other person by allowing him or her to experience for a lifetime the benefits of your compassion without being expected to make a similar response. God's desire is that this person also grows into a compassionate, responsible individual. If your partner's response of compassion toward you is strikingly less than yours, he or she may stagnate at that point and not be challenged to grow into a more loving person. Don't expect that your influence or marriage itself will change your partner. The most compassionate thing you can do for this person is not to marry him or her.

If, however, compassion is strong on both sides of your relationship, rejoice! If it is matched with compatibility at other points which we'll look at, you have a sound basis to proceed with marriage.

7
Are You
Good
Friends?

◆◆◆◆◆

One of the most essential principles in considering marriage is so basic it can elude you. Is there a solid basis of friendship in your relationship? Do you enjoy being together and relating together in a creative variety of ways?

This isn't to say that friendship alone assures a good marriage. Friendship may be based on factors that don't build the two of you up and strengthen your relationship to Christ. You don't have to look beyond Scripture to find many examples of couples who led each other down the primrose path.

Yet when friendship is mixed with compassion and Christian maturity, you have a solid foundation for marriage. As with compassion, though, it's easy to overlook the significance of friendship in looking for more dramatic indications of romantic love. Friendship may seem too unspectacular a basis for marriage. Hollywood has programmed us to think of romantic love as something dramatically different from friendship—even the antithesis of friendship.

Consider the theme we see so frequently: A man and woman who are antagonists suddenly find themselves inexplicably attracted to each other. A fiery, passionate relationship ensues and they live happily ever after. Thus the expression "Love and hate are the same emotions, different names."

But while this theme makes for good entertainment, and definitely appeals to our sense of adventure, it spells disaster for marriage. It's simply naive to think that romantic chemistry will triumph over all the problems of incompatibility in a relationship. In reality, the day-to-day demands of marriage are such that unless two people enjoy being together in many ways besides the romantic, the relationship will not likely endure.

On the other hand, when friendship is strong, there is a solid foundation for romance to grow, even within the most stressful conditions of family life. I challenge you to look carefully at any marriage relationship which impresses you. Talk to the couple. You will undoubtedly find that at the basis of the relationship is a strong and enduring friendship which could well survive apart from the marriage. In *Till Death Do Us Part,* researchers Robert and Jeanette Lauer aptly note, "Successful couples regard their spouses as friends, the kind of person they would want to have as a friend even if they weren't married to them."[1]

I'm aware of many excellent marriages, also, which began as good friendships with no romantic expectations. In some cases it took quite a while for interest in marriage to blossom. The point is crucial to keep in mind, for we're programmed to think that marriage love more typically occurs at first sight. That belief can hinder you from giving a friendship a fair chance to develop into something more. Many, in search of some romantic ideal, never realize the potential that exists in a friendship they already have.

Of course, the positive side is that the seeds for a good marriage may be present in a friendship you now have, even though neither of you has thought about it. Again, remember the survey we noted in chapter three: one thousand happily married people were interviewed. A full eighty percent admitted they had not at first been attracted romantically to the one who became their spouse. It suggests that love at first sight—especially genuine, dynamic marriage-love—is the definite exception, not the rule.

With each passing year I come more and more to appreciate how rare genuine, lasting friendship actually is. As a young person, I took friendship very much for granted. Now I'm embarrassed to admit how many friendships which seemed so significant at the time have fallen by the wayside. I count those which have endured as pearls of great price. If you have a deep, trusting friendship with someone of the opposite sex, count it as an extraordinary gift. It may or may not be a basis for marriage. But don't be too quick to dismiss the possibility just because romantic chemistry isn't yet there.

Priscilla and Aquila

It's striking that most biblical pictures of married couples are negative. When you search the Scriptures for examples of married individuals who had a redemptive influence on one another, you find them few and far between. Remarkably, in the New Testament Priscilla and Aquila are the only couple shown in a positive light at any length after Pentecost. What is most apparent from the passages that mention them is that more than anything else they were good friends.

Their friendship stretched to numerous areas. For one thing, they were in business together, as tentmakers (Acts 18:3). I doubt there is any greater test of friendship than the ability to work together in a common trade. The sheer amount of time spent together quickly takes the edge of novelty off any relationship. The potential for ego conflicts, annoyance over each other's idiosyncrasies, disagreement over finances and plain boredom is enormous. Yet the quality of their friendship even in this challenging environment was such that Paul himself was drawn into camaraderie with them and became a fellow partner in their work. In time their congeniality opened them to friendships with personalities as diverse as Apollos (Acts 18:24-28) and Timothy (2 Tim 4:19).

We also know that they traveled extensively and established homes in several regions. In the mere six passages which mention them, they are referred to in several different locales, including Rome, Corinth, Syria and Ephesus (Acts 18:1-3, 18, 24-28; Rom 16:3-5). When Paul wished to leave Corinth for Syria, they picked up and went with him. Considering the extreme travel conditions of the day, they had a most impressive sense of adventure. They enjoyed tackling challenges together, the bigger the better.

Of special interest is the fact that they formed churches in their homes. They shared not only business but pastoral responsibilities as well. They also studied together, grew intellectually together and exercised such a significant counseling ministry together that Apollos, a Billy Graham figure of the first century, was greatly influenced by their constructive criticism (Acts 18:24-28).

What I find most interesting is the fact that Priscilla's name is mentioned first in four of the six references to them (Acts 18:18, 26; Rom 16:3-4; 2 Tim 4:19). This suggests that she was more publicly visible and probably regarded as the more gifted of the two. This also tells us that Aquila was not intimidated by Priscilla using her gifts and having a certain limelight of her own. He probably even encouraged her to cultivate and use her gifts. He must have been an unbelievably supportive husband, particularly considering the demeaning views held toward women in the first century. Perhaps more than anything this signifies the depth of their friendship and the level of compassion which Aquila felt toward his marriage partner.

The New Testament says nothing of romantic love between Priscilla and Aquila, though we can guess it was probably there. But whether or not they loved each other romantically, one thing is clear: they *liked* each other. I don't think we can overemphasize the importance of the fact that the Holy Spirit, in recording but one positive example of a married couple in the New Testament church, gave such attention to factors in their friendship.

Assessing Your Friendship

But what does this mean for your own relationship? On one level judging friendship is easy enough. You instinctively know when the bond of friendship exists with someone and don't need anyone's formula for figuring that out. Yet determining whether your friendship has the qualities which would make for a good marriage can be more challenging. Let me suggest some guidelines for weighing this:

Do you have a variety of common interests? A friendship can develop because of a common involvement in one area. You might be drawn to someone in a drama club, for instance, because of your mutual love for acting. But if that attraction dries up or becomes impractical to pursue, will there be enough other areas to keep your relationship strong and on the growing edge? I don't mean that you must share all interests in common. It will be important for each of you to have individual pursuits as well. Yet you shouldn't consider marriage unless you have at least several significant points of common interest.

How well do you support each other at your points of strength? Do you find it natural to encourage the other to develop and use his or her gifts, even if these are not ones that you personally have? Does he or she find it natural to encourage you in this way? The way I've phrased the question is not accidental. I did not ask, "Are you willing to do this?" but "Do you find it *natural* to do so?" One of the most beautiful aspects of friendship is the way in which two people inspire each other to be the best they can be, helping the other always to appear in the best possible light. This is a vital dynamic for a marriage relationship.

How comfortable are you accepting the other's humanness and weaknesses? If you're thinking, "My partner doesn't have any significant problems or idiosyncrasies which I find annoying," you clearly don't know that person well enough to get married! In close friendship two people become acquainted well enough to find that neither is a plaster of Paris saint—each has qualities which are less than admirable. Yet friends find it natural to forgive and overlook many offensives. A missed phone call, a late arrival, a thoughtless remark, while irritating at the time, doesn't become a source of long-term contention. Friends instinctively realize that the good outweighs the bad in a relationship, and that it's not worth accentuating the negative to the point that the positive is overshadowed.

Though you've undoubtedly heard it said many times, marriage is not likely to change things which you don't like about your partner. If the other has a characteristic which you'd find unbearable to live with, then you should definitely not consider marriage. On the other hand, if you're comfortable accepting the other at the point of his or her roughest edges, even finding them laughable at times, then you have one of the most cherished qualities of friendship.

How often do you laugh together? Is there a lighthearted side to your relationship? Are you able to take good-natured teasing from each other, and others as well?

Just this week, a woman who has been through a marriage breakup told me that one of the most difficult parts of the relationship was the fact that her husband lacked a sense of humor. He couldn't laugh at himself.

In his insightful book *Love Is Not Enough,* Sol Gordon advises, "If it is extremely difficult for you to develop a sense of humor, please do not plan on raising a family; laughter is a compulsory ingredient when it comes to having children."[2] I would go practically as far in speaking of the relationship between husband and wife itself. While a sense of humor may not be the most essential aspect of a healthy marriage, it's far from the least significant. With Dr. Gordon I would rate it as more important even than sexual attraction.[3]

Do you build each other up in Christ? Again, friendships come in healthy and unhealthy varieties, as Scripture constantly shows. Overall, do you build each other up in Christ and encourage each other's spiritual growth? (We will look at this issue in greater detail in chapter eleven.)

Are you likely to enjoy carrying out marriage responsibilities together? Picture yourself doing the things you will have to do together in family life—raising children, maintaining a home, carrying out the endless assortment of domestic chores. Do these tasks seem like activities that would be enjoyable to do together or routines that must be tolerated to enjoy the physical side of the relationship or some other factor that may be drawing you together? Be honest. Over the years about ninety-five per cent of your time together will be spent in domestic responsibilities, not in romantic intimacy. While of necessity these cannot always be scintillating tasks, you should at least have a general desire to share this area of life together.

What about the physical side of friendship? You can, of course, have a deep and lasting friendship with someone of the opposite sex in which no physical attraction is present. But in a relationship which has prospects for marriage, you will naturally be concerned about the potential for eros. Here several things should be kept in mind.

1. Physical attraction can come at a later point, even when it isn't present at the beginning of a friendship. If other factors in your relationship are good, and if at least the *possibility* of physical attraction is there, allow reasonable time for it to develop. Again, remember that most of us have to go through considerable deprogramming of unreasonable ideals in this area before we can enter into a physical relationship that is truly healthy.

2. The physical relationship is not the panacea in marriage it's often thought to be. In speaking of reasons to consider marriage, Sol Gordon notes aptly, "Frankly, sex alone is not worth it."[4] Remember that most of your time in marriage will be spent in other activities. If in all honesty the main focus of your concern and energy in the relationship is on the physical, then other aspects of friendship are probably not strong enough to recommend marriage.

3. The level of physical attraction which you feel for each other may not have to be as overwhelming as you think to provide the basis for a good marriage. (This point is so important that I'll devote considerable attention to it in chapter nine.)

Beware of unreasonable ideals. Be careful of holding the friendship up to unrealistic expectations. Pastor and author Larry Richards speaks of a woman whom he knew who divorced her husband because their marriage was only "ninety percent good." For her, nothing less than perfection was acceptable; she left a ninety percent relationship to search for one that was one hundred percent perfect.[5] Her attitude was not only naive but tragically self-defeating. For most of us, some revision of our expectations will be needed at virtually every point if we are to find a fulfilling marriage relationship.

Be especially cautious in comparing your present relationship with others you've had. While some comparing of this sort is usually unavoidable (all valuative thinking involves comparisons), it's easy to reach misleading conclusions. It's quite possible that a past relationship was more electrifying or dynamic in some particular way than your present one. It's all too easy, too, to overglamorize past relationships (or imagined future ones) and to miss the potential in a present one. Treat this relationship as an entity in itself. If it measures up well against the guidelines I'm suggesting, and if compassion between you is strong, you may well have an excellent foundation for marriage.

Friendship is a remarkable gift of God and one of the greatest luxuries of life which he allows us to enjoy. In marriage it is not merely a luxury but essential to fulfillment and fruitfulness on every level. Keep it high on your list of considerations in weighing the possibility of marriage. Indeed, much of the secret to a good marriage is to marry a friend.

8

Are You Both
Ready
for Marriage?

◆▬◆▬◆

I n my first year of seminary I fell into the habit of arriving a few
minutes late for a particular class. The professor called me into his
office one day and told me bluntly that he was annoyed with the
practice. Since he suspected that I was eager for marriage, he added,
"If you ever want to be married, you had better learn to be more
punctual—your wife will find it intolerable to live with someone who
can't manage time."

I had honestly never thought of it this way before. I was still quite
naive in my thinking about marriage and assumed that love and being
Christian would cover any problems that arose. Now it is only too clear
that the professor was right. Maturity and lifestyle factors make an

enormous difference in the ability of two people to live effectively together in marriage. In considering your compatibility with someone, it's as important to look carefully at how ready both of you are for marriage.

Judging Your Readiness for Marriage

The question of values. Do you both accept the biblical teaching that marriage is forever? There are many in our society who look upon marriage as an experimental option ("if it doesn't work, I'll get out"), and it's hard not to be affected by this mentality. If there's even the slightest thought in either of your minds of approaching the marriage experimentally, don't go ahead.

How much personal worth do each of you have tied up in making the marriage work? It's vital that each of you has a strong ego need to be part of an enduring marriage. It should be a significant matter of personal pride to see the marriage succeed. If either of you is at all indifferent about this, if the thought of the marriage ever breaking up seems less than devastating to you, then your motivation for a lifetime commitment is less than it needs to be.

It's important, too, not only to look at what each other's values are, but also at why you hold them. There are many less than sufficient reasons why we may buy into certain values: we inherit them from parents, absorb them from our Christian culture, go along with them to be accepted by others, believe them simply because they are "right." God gives us standards to live by because he understands much better than we do what will contribute to our long-term well-being. But unless we are convinced on the deepest level that we really will be happier following them than going our own way, they will have little holding power when the chips are down.

We've all seen cases of those who carry their values on their sleeves—preaching to others about the need for faithfulness in marriage—who cave in themselves when a sufficient enticement comes along. When you scratch beneath the surface, you usually find that they were holding their values unreflectively without really under-standing why they were necessary.

Family history. While we are not fated to inherit the life-patterns of our parents, they do form a certain default mode in our experience. If both sets of parents have had good marriages, the prospects of your own marriage being successful are enhanced. If parents of either have divorced, separated or had a difficult marriage, there's a greater than normal chance of that pattern repeating if certain stress factors occur in your marriage. If either of you is the child of an unhappy marriage, you need to be sure that you understand the factors that led to your parents' problems. It's vital that you have the self-understand-ing and determination to avoid the same destructive pattern. Here counseling is usually essential.

Track records. What sort of success have you each had in keeping commitments in other areas of life—jobs, dedication to projects, past friendships and relationships? Is the evidence really there that you have the maturity to keep a commitment as enduring as marriage?

The age question. While the question of age is somewhat subjective, the odds are greatly in your favor if both of you are at least into your twenties. One study showed that divorces in American families where both married under the age of twenty-one were six times the national average.[1] In the island community where I go to write, thirteen of a flock of fifteen high-school marriages ended in divorce. I strongly recommend waiting until each of you is at least twenty-one before marrying.

How much experience have you each had living independently? This is a more significant issue than the age question. It's normally unwise to marry before each has lived at a full responsibility level independent of parents for at least several years.

"For this reason a man will leave his father and mother and be united to his wife, and they will become one flesh" (Gen 2:24). If you feel compelled to go on living with a parent, you're definitely not ready for marriage. I'm not speaking here of the special situation where you decide (as a mature, free choice) to care for an infirm parent or relative, and you and your partner both agree on doing this. Though this often creates a highly stressful situation for a young couple, it can be a workable one. However, if either of you feels bound to continue living with a parent for security reasons, or from fear of disappointing the parent, then you don't own your own life sufficiently to enter marriage.

Of course, leaving parents means more than physical separation. You can live five thousand miles from your folks and still be strongly under the control of their expectations. While Scripture enjoins us always to honor our parents, we are called as adults to freely manage our own lives so that we may submit them in freedom to Christ. If you find it greatly difficult to say no to a parent, or are easily swayed by their wishes which go against your better judgment, you don't own your life adequately to give of yourself in marriage. I heartily recommend getting Harold Halpern's excellent book *Cutting Loose: An Adult Guide for Coming to Terms with Parents*. [2] Read it thoroughly, carefully consider the points he raises and where appropriate follow his suggestions for gaining healthy (but respectful) independence from your parents before thinking further about marriage.[3]

How well do you manage time? My professor was right—good handling of your time is vital to effective functioning in marriage. No one can be punctual all of the time, emergencies do occur, and none of us ever perfectly manages the time which we have. Yet if either of you is frequently late, cannot be depended upon to keep a commitment or has difficulty saying no to someone in order to keep a commitment already made to someone else, you have a serious problem with managing time. You'll not only have difficulty holding down employment, but also in being an effective helpmate to your partner in marriage.

Fortunately poor time management is a treatable ailment (I'm a case in point). Through making the effort, each of us can achieve greater discipline and gain greater control of our use of time. A book or seminar on time management can help. But if time management is a significant problem for either of you, don't think about going forward with marriage at this time. Deal with this problem first. Then allow at least six months of consistent improvement to demonstrate to yourself and your partner that genuine change has taken place.

Don't be fooled into thinking that marriage will cure the problems either of you has with managing time. If anything, it will make matters worse. Contrary to popular fancies, marriage doesn't bestow on us a magical ability to rise above time. The day-to-day realities of marriage are lived out *within* time. Thus, proper management of time is essential to a healthy marriage.

How well do you manage money? My question here is not whether you agree on what your standard of living should be (an issue we'll look at in chapter twelve), but how well you live within the means that you actually have. None of us is perfect in our handling of money. Yet if either of you frequently outspends your income or has trouble paying bills or keeping financial commitments, then you're probably not ready for the increased financial burdens of marriage.

I make this point less dogmatically than the others, for the division of financial responsibility varies from marriage to marriage, and couples sometimes balance out each other's strong and weak points in this area. But it's vital that you look together at how you will manage money in marriage and grade yourself on how well this is likely to be done. If your mark is not a high one, then you should get help in learning how to manage finances before going ahead with marriage. A college course in home economics, a seminar on financial management or sessions with a financial consultant may help.

Are you emotionally ready to forsake the benefits of the single life? Many who marry in their college or high school years, and some who marry well into adulthood, discover that they are not nearly as ready to let go of the advantages of singleness as they thought. Though the prospect of marriage was alluring, once the newness wears off they find themselves restless and longing for the freedom of movement they enjoyed before becoming attached. Not a few marriages break up over this tension.

Personalities vary greatly, as does the timing of individual growth, and some are ready to make the transition from singleness to marriage at a much earlier age than others. It is important that you each know yourself well enough to judge whether you are truly ready to make the trade-offs involved. Especially if you or your partner are in your early twenties or below, I strongly recommend exploring the question thoroughly with a qualified counselor. Make sure you are not pushing yourself beyond reasonable limits in making this leap.

Length of acquaintance. Again, individuals and relationships differ widely, and it is impossible to lay down a rigid formula for acquaintance time before marriage. Some couples are able to make a mature decision about marriage in a fairly short period of time while others need several years or more to work things through. Generally it is advisable to allow at least a year for getting acquainted before you move into marriage. I suggest this not only because it usually takes this much time to get to know someone well enough to forge a lifetime commitment, but also because we are all seasonal creatures to some extent. It is important to understand how seasonal differences may affect both your individual personality patterns and the dynamics of your relationship.

Have you had the chance to observe each other under difficult conditions? Much more important than the length of acquaintance is the quality of it. A friend who endured a difficult marriage breakup confessed to me, "Before marriage we always saw each other on our best time." Marriage brought with it unexpected revelations about each other's character. It's true that in dating you tend to see each other under optimum conditions that bear little resemblance to the stresses of marriage. It can be hard to gauge what personality patterns will be like in the day-to-day realities of married life. (This is another reason that relationships which begin as friendships with no romantic pretenses often provide the best basis for marriage.)

Before entering marriage, it's important to have reasonable opportunities for observing how each other responds to stress, including major disappointments or failures and day-to-day annoyances, such as getting stuck in traffic. Is the typical reaction a flash of anger, whining or withdrawal? Or is there the ability to rise above the situation and show congeniality and optimism even when frustrated? And how do you each respond when disappointed with the other? Is there a tendency to berate or belittle the other? Or does an atmosphere of forgiveness and constructive discussion more typically prevail?

I would strongly caution against marrying anyone who has poor emotional control. Here let me be especially clear in explaining what I mean. Anyone will lose their temper on occasion or react to disappointment in a less than commendable way. The mature person will later apologize, show remorse and make some effort to avoid repeating the pattern. The immature person will tend to prolong the response, wallowing in anger or self-pity, and may not apologize or make any meaningful effort to improve. I don't mean there is no hope that this person can change and grow. But until that happens, he or she shouldn't be considered a candidate for marriage.

Run, do not walk, away from a relationship with anyone who is in any way physically abusive to you—slapping, kicking, punching, pushing. (It's more common in Christian relationships than you think.) Under no condition—short of very clear and sustained evidence of reform through counseling should you consider marrying such a person.

Are You Both Free of Chemical Addictions? Under no circumstances should you consider marrying someone who has an active addiction to drugs or alcohol. You will buy into a lifetime of hell if you do. Don't bank on promises of reform or pledges to seek treatment being fulfilled. Even when made with the very best intentions, addicts more often renege on these than carry through. If the addict does seek help or renounce the habit, you should allow at least a full year of unaddicted behavior with no relapses to pass as evidence that genuine recovery has taken place before considering marriage to this person.

Are either of you desperate to get married? Do you feel that life will have no purpose if you can't get married? Are you expecting marriage to solve major personal problems? If so, then the marriage is headed for trouble before it starts. I don't mean that it's wrong to hope that marriage will improve your life; without that hope there's little sense in getting married. But I'm speaking of balance here. Unless you are reasonably content with the direction of your life apart from being married, you will lack the strength of character to be a supportive partner in marriage. As hard as it is to accept, you will do yourself and the other a great favor by putting off marriage.

I would recommend, too, reading and studying at least one book dealing with the problem of addictive or unhealthy love. There are some excellent ones to choose from, noted in the footnote below.[4] Give close thought to what really makes for healthy marriage love, and take the steps needed to grow to the point where you can give and receive this kind of affection. In the end you'll not only be a happier person, but a much more effective marriage partner as well.

Toss Your Rose-Colored Glasses Aside

But how is it possible to get a realistic picture of each other in the rose-colored-glasses atmosphere of dating? It can take some effort. One way is to plan some activities together which will put you in more challenging social situations. Some suggestions:

☐ Go on a ski trip or backpacking expedition with singles from your church.

☐ Plan a weekend visit to parents or relatives who live out of town.

☐ Go on a short-term missions project together (a particularly good option from many angles).

☐ Commit yourself to weekly service together in an inner-city ministry or nursing home.

Additionally, don't hesitate to talk with friends, family members or work associates of your partner and, where it can be done discreetly, ask them for an honest evaluation of that person's character and potential as a marriage partner. If this sounds conniving, remember that you are looking at spending the rest of your life with this person. If you were hiring someone for a business, you wouldn't hesitate to get references, even for someone engaged for a short-term project. How much more important it may be to do this for the most binding commitment you'll ever have to make.

The Value of Counseling

As important as the issues raised in this chapter are, I realize that judging yourself or your partner at any of these points can be easier said than done. Some of us tend to be too lenient in such judgments, others too harsh. If there is any question how clearly you are seeing things, the importance of getting counsel from someone who is qualified to help with the marriage decision can scarcely be overemphasized. Seek the best professional help available in your area, even if it means paying a reasonable fee for services. The amount you pay for sessions with a marriage counselor will probably be a drop in the bucket compared to the investment you've already made in education for your career.

I urge you, too, to go through a series of sessions in premarital counseling once you become engaged. Just recently a friend admitted to me: "my wife and I never had premarital counseling. We didn't take our first personality survey until we were four or five years into our marriage. Premarital counseling would have saved us a lot of headaches."

The pastor who marries you may offer such service (and some insist upon it), but many do not. And while some take the process quite seriously, others mete out rather cursory advice in their sessions. Again, take advantage of the best help that is available in your area, even if it means seeking out a professional who specializes in family counseling. Marriage is too serious a step to do otherwise.

9

Are You
Physically
Compatible?

▲ ▲ ▲ ▲ ▲

Don and Jean dated for three years, but had broken up several months before asking to talk with me. Both were mature, congenial Christians in their later twenties. Both held responsible jobs and were making good strides in their careers. In meeting with me separately, each stressed how much they cared for the other and how significant their friendship had been. Each had dreamed often of marrying the other, and at most points they seemed an ideal match. It was the issue of physical compatibility that was holding them back.

Don feared that his sexual attraction to Jean wasn't strong enough to justify marriage. "I simply don't feel the electricity in this relationship which I thought I'd experience when the right person came along—or that I know I'm capable of feeling," he explained. Jean also wondered if her physical attraction to Don was strong enough for marriage. Yet her greater concern was with Don's ambivalence toward her. She found it demeaning to think of marrying someone who was less than moonstruck over her.

At the same time each insisted that they were sexually attracted to each other, to the point that control had been difficult at times. The problem was not the absence of eros but the fact that each fell short of the other's ideals.

Don and Jean's example is typical of Christian couples I've known who expressed similar confusion to me about the physical factor in relationships. The most common question asked by Christian men, in fact, is how intense sexual attraction must be to justify marriage. Many, like Don, fear that their physical attraction to someone whom they're otherwise quite compatible with isn't strong enough for marriage. Women sometimes raise the question too. More typically, though, their concern is like Jean's—whether to marry a boyfriend who has confessed that his sexual feelings are only moderate, or that he still finds it possible to be attracted to other women. This seems to fall so short of the childhood dream of someone who'll cherish you as his only true love.

These concerns are only too understandable. The hope for sexual pleasure is not only a major motive for marriage, but the physical relationship itself is, for most of us, the highest symbol of unity and perfection in marriage. We fear any compromise that might jeopardize our happiness or suggest that the marriage is less than fully blessed by God. But while the physical relationship is important, many Christians place too much importance upon it. Some are looking for an intensity of attraction that isn't reasonable or healthy to expect. Others have unreasonable expectations about how their partner should feel about them.

After meeting only once with Don and Jean each, I was persuaded that each was holding onto ideals that were neither realistic nor likely to contribute to their happiness in marriage, and I told them so. I was convinced, too, that they were a strongly compatible couple and that underneath they really did want to marry each other. While I was careful to stress that I wasn't giving them a divine oracle, I did tell them that I thought they'd do well to marry. It was the greatest joy of my life when a week later they announced their engagement. They've been married over two years now and are doing well.

Don and Jean bring me hope as I treat this topic, for I'm reminded that there are many who want to be shown where their ideals are unrealistic. They instinctively realize the importance of Christ's teaching that truth, and not fantasy, sets us free. It is hard to grow up in American society and not to carry at least some sense that your perspective on love and romance is being shaped more by myth than by reality. Yet, there is a dearth of clear teaching on this subject in the body of Christ. So for those with ears to hear it, let me now say it emphatically: *This is an area where our thinking tends to be formed much more by Hollywood ideas and popular Christianity than by Scripture and common sense.* Certain myths about the physical relationship prevail, even within the body of Christ, and keep many from clear thinking about the marriage choice.

Myths about Physical Compatibility

Myth 1: Sexual attraction must be overwhelming before you decide to marry someone. Many assume that when they've met the one they are to marry, the sexual attraction between them will be strong enough to fuel the neon lights of Las Vegas. Whatever is meant by the notion of "romantic love," this is usually more at the heart of it than anything. This belief leaves many like Don, who find themselves in a good relationship where eros is less intense than they thought it should be, confused. Others wait endlessly for that ecstatic relationship that never seems to come.

Scripture does teach that sexual attraction is important in marriage. As we have noted, in 1 Corinthians 7:1-7 Paul goes as far as to say that apart from a significant sexual need, one shouldn't marry. Paul's clear implication, too, is that two people considering marriage should desire to fulfill their sexual needs with each other. Interestingly, though, Paul never addresses the question of how strong sexual attraction must be to justify marriage.

Elsewhere Paul says, "For this is the will of God, your sanctification: that you abstain from immorality; that each one of you know how to take a wife for himself in holiness and honor, not in the passion of lust like heathen who do not know God" (1 Thess 4:3-5 RSV). Thus, sexual attraction can reach a level where it overrides good judgement and interferes with sensitivity in other areas of a relationship. When this is considered along with the 1 Corinthians passage, it becomes clear that eros does not have to be volcanic to make for a good marriage.

Experience shows that the best marriages are often those where *moderate* physical attraction exists along with strong compassion, friendship and compatibility at other points. When eros is overwhelming, it can become obsessive and a block to growth and compatibility in other areas. The effect of extreme sexual attraction is not unlike that of a drug addiction. Your life revolves around the moment of physical encounter. The ninety-five percent of married life which must be spent apart from the physical relationship becomes dull and unstimulating. You find it hard to be compassionate and sensitive toward your partner when he or she isn't interested in making love.

Those, too, who enter marriage with unreasonably high expectations for the sexual relationship are in the greatest danger of a letdown. If the couple hasn't nurtured other areas of interest, the marriage is headed for disaster before it starts. In the end it is the balance, or combination, of factors that makes for a happy and healthy marriage.

Myth 2: You will be more strongly attracted sexually to the person you are to marry than you've ever been toward anyone else. While this is true in some cases, it isn't in many others. Most of us are so constituted that we can experience sexual feelings—even very strong attraction—for virtually anyone of the opposite sex who fits certain stereotypes which we have been conditioned to find appealing. This includes many who would make anything but a good marriage partner for us.

To say it more specifically, it is possible that you have had a past relationship where eros ran stronger than it does in your present one. That is not a reason in itself to conclude that your present relationship is unfit for marriage. You may not have been as well matched at other points in the past relationship as you are now. Remember that it's always misleading to compare a single feature of relationships. Look at the combination of factors in your present relationship and see what it suggests. Remember, too, that we tend to overglamorize past relationships—to remember the happy moments and forget the difficult parts. Look at your present relationship as an entity in itself.

Myth 3: If either of you still finds it possible to be physically attracted to anyone else, then you aren't cut out for marriage to each other. I've known individuals who claim that they've never been physically attracted to anyone but their spouse. I find them, though, to be the rare exception (and possibly less than fully honest at that). Most of us do have the potential to feel sexual desire for more than one person, even at the same time. It is the nature of erotic desire that it can be invested in a variety of directions, a point that Paul seems to have well in mind in 1 Corinthians 7. When he advises Christians to marry "because there is so much immorality," his point is not, "marry the one person who attracts you so strongly that you can't think of anyone else," but "because of the possibility of multiple attractions, determine to invest your sexual energies in one person, *your spouse.*" This doesn't change the fact that I may be naturally inclined to be attracted to others, but it does underline the crucial need for commitment and determination not to let my interests stray outside of the marriage relationship.

Those in relationships like Don and Jean's often feel hurt and disillusioned when the other admits to having wandering fancies at times. Like Jean, they wonder whether God could want them to marry someone who even finds it possible to be attracted to someone else.

My advice to those in Jean's situation, though, is to look more at your partner's ability and willingness to be committed to you than at the more intangible matter of whether his or her fantasies ever wander. In the long run it is his or her determination to stay loyal to you that will make the difference, not whether their feelings ever run in other directions.

Be grateful, too, for your partner's honesty. Realize that most people in serious relationships have the same variety of feelings which your partner has confessed. They simply are not as honest in admitting it.

Of course, usually the hardest part is dealing with your own self-esteem. In our hearts we each want to know that someone else loves us so greatly that the possibility of another affection never enters their mind. It's a blow to our pride to find that the reality of things is less than this. But ultimately our security must be in Christ and not in another person, not even our spouse. Only as I can come to rest in knowing that Christ loves me as though I were the only person in existence, as Augustine put it, will I be able to fully enjoy a relationship with another human being whose capacity to love can never be as perfect as this. It's through security in Christ that I can let go of childhood fantasies about romance and enjoy the reality of a marriage relationship for what it is.

Myth 4: Your physical attraction for the one you marry will never waver. Again this is an unfortunate misnomer which simply ignores human nature. Both during courtship and during marriage itself there will be an ebb and flow to physical desire on the part of both of you. The important thing is not how you feel on a given hour or day but the pattern of attraction over a period of time.

Myth 5: You will know instantly or early on in a relationship whether physical attraction can be experienced. This is perhaps the most misleading notion of all, for it keeps many relationships with good potential from having the chance to develop. It's an unfortunate side of our love-at-first-sight myth. To an important extent physical attraction can be learned and developed, especially when compassion and friendship are already strong. While you shouldn't consider marriage if no eros is present, neither should you be too quick to conclude that it can never develop. Physical attraction that develops after friendship already exists is often more enduring than that which forms apart from friendship and so often becomes the main basis for a relationship. Unless friendship keeps pace, the physical flame eventually dies out.

Judging Physical Compatibility

But how do you actually know that you and another person will enjoy sex together in marriage? The answer is that you can trust your instincts. Here it is perhaps necessary to refute yet another myth—the idea that you must experiment to find out if you are physically compatible with someone else. Throughout biblical times and for centuries thereafter, excellent marriages were arranged by parents, who instinctively recognized that their sons or daughters would be physically compatible with someone else. In many cases, too, matchmakers filled the same function and were remarkably successful. If an outside party under the guidance of God can determine this for someone, without any direct evidence that the marriage will work, then certainly we who follow Christ can make this judgment for ourselves.

If you have gotten to know someone well, and you can imagine that you would enjoy sexual relations with this person in marriage, you can trust that insight as being as reliable as any discovery that would come from prolonged experimentation, if not more so. Rather than preach to you on the virtues of abstinence (which I could certainly do), let me simply encourage you to leave as much as possible in the physical arena to look forward to in marriage. This will add a greater dimension of joy to the early days of your life together.

I'm not denying that either of you may have inhibitions or attitudes which will interfere with a healthy sex life in marriage. Yet these can be discovered as well through discussion as through physical involvement before marriage. If these do exist, by all means get counseling and work them through before entering a lifetime of intimate relations.

Remember that God wills your success and happiness in marriage. As you look to him for wisdom, you can trust that he is giving you sound insight as you dream of the future and discuss this area together.

The Question of Frequency

The question remains whether it is necessary to have clear agreement before marriage on how frequently and when you will have sex. While I would strongly encourage you to talk about this, it's frankly impossible to predict what precisely your sexual needs will be at different points in marriage. Your sex drive will be affected considerably by a multitude of factors, including rest, health, age, weather, time of year, (for women) point in the menstrual cycle, work pressures, family stresses and last but far from least, the state of your self-esteem.

It's extremely unlikely that both of you will always find your level of interest in the physical relationship to be at the same point. In a normal relationship there will be more times when one is eager and the other not than when both are equally inclined. Paul is straightforward in saying that when husband and wife are at different states of desire, preference should be given to the one with the sexual need (1 Cor 7:4-5). Again, we come back to the crucial elements of compassion, friendship and maturity in marriage, for each needs to be ready and willing to accommodate the other sexually even when desire is one-sided.

At the same time, compassion is a two-way street. Each should be willing to bridle his or her desire at times out of consideration for the other's state of interest. Over time you discover that sex is far and away most enjoyable when both strongly desire it. Quality is far more important than frequency. As you come to appreciate this, it becomes easier to exercise restraint and to plan love-making for the most favorable time.

What it boils down to is the need for a lot of give-and-take in the physical relationship—times when one accommodates the other, times when one restrains out of respect for the other's feelings, times when you agree together to set aside a special time for being intimate. As you think of the future, it's not so important to agree now on a schedule for intimacy as to determine if the openness to this give-and-take is really there. Again, it comes down to compassion—the determination to will the other's best. This is the most essential ingredient for lasting physical compatibility in marriage.

What If Eros Is Overwhelming?

I've been discussing relationships in which individuals are uncertain about whether physical attraction is strong enough for marriage. I realize, however, that some readers have quite the opposite concern! You may be in one where physical attraction runs very strong and wonder whether it's O.K. to marry with the velocity of eros this high. Or you may wonder how any other alternative besides marriage could possibly be considered given the intensity of your feelings.

Some Christians assume that they are virtually obligated to get married in this situation, given Paul's admonition (1 Cor 7) to seek marriage as a refuge against the temptation of having sex out of wedlock. Keep in mind, however, that Paul also warns against letting the physical factor alone draw you into marriage (1 Thess 4:3-5). When the overall biblical teaching on marriage is understood, it is quite clear that a number of factors besides eros need to line up before marriage is recommended.

If you are in a relationship where sexual attraction is especially strong, I cannot urge you strongly enough to make every effort to keep your head in thinking through the possibility of marriage. Err on the side of caution in allowing adequate time to get acquainted. Look at the other compatibility factors and carefully consider how well you match up at these points. Also, seek out a qualified counselor and meet with that person individually and then together. Thoroughly explore with him or her the question of how fully compatible for marriage you actually are.

It is certainly possible that you will discover that you match up well at other points besides the physical. The fact that you are strongly attracted physically does not in itself recommend against marriage anymore than it recommends for it. However, if you find that your overall compatibility is not strong enough to recommend marriage, you will need to take one of the most difficult steps anyone ever has to take. You will need to decide either not to go ahead with marriage or at least to shelve that possibility until your relationship has the chance to grow and season in other areas. As painful as that choice will be, it will be far less painful than entering a lifetime union that cannot possibly deliver what it seems to promise.

10
Are You Intellectually Compatible?

▲▲▲▲▲

I went through a phase as a young Christian in which I assumed that the woman I married should be a musical performer like myself. I was director of a music ministry at the time, and so much of my life was wrapped up in this work that it seemed hard to imagine being married to someone without the same level of involvement in it. To say the least, this assumption limited my options considerably.

A wise older friend one day suggested that my marriage might be happier and more balanced if my wife didn't share my intensive interest in music. I look back on that conversation now as one of the most important turning points in my thinking about marriage, for it broadened my thinking and opened me to new possibilities.

While Evie, the woman I married several years later, did have a background in music education, she wasn't a performer, and our interests in music were quite different. Yet I discovered the truth of my friend's advice during the first year of marriage, for it provided a welcome retreat from the fast lane environment of the music ministry. With Evie I was able to turn off the stresses of the work and return to it refreshed. I suspect this wouldn't have happened as well had I been married to another performer.

Like other areas of compatibility which we're looking at, intellectual compatibility is one where our thinking easily gets clouded by myth and unreasonable ideals. While intellectual compatibility between a husband and wife is clearly important, defining what constitutes it in a given relationship is a delicate question. In my own case it was necessary to let go of an unfortunate assumption before I could find a truly compatible relationship.

I find Christians today obsessed with the concern for intellectual compatibility in marriage. While I'm sure this has always been a factor among those thinking about marriage, there are two trends which make this a unique obsession of our time. One is the rise in educational level and professional standing among women. If you look at marriages of those a generation or two beyond you, you find many examples of happy marriages in which the husband is college-educated, even with multiple degrees, while the wife never went beyond high school. Because the cultural pattern encouraged education and professional advancement among men and discouraged it among women, intellectual equality in marriage was not a major issue.

Today, of course, the cultural tide has changed considerably. While sexism remains a problem at times, women generally are encouraged to strive for their full potential and feel under considerable pressure to do so. As the lines of distinction between men and women become blurred in more and more educational and professional areas, both men and women come more and more to expect the person they marry to be their intellectual and creative match.

The other factor which makes intellectual compatibility a greater concern is the later age at which people tend to marry. It has become much more acceptable to be a professional single, especially in urban areas, and many purposely choose to delay marriage until they have finished their education and launched their career. Though this contributes to greater maturity at the time of marriage, it also makes the matter of finding a compatible relationship more challenging, at least from the standpoint of expectations. With each year of life your wisdom and experience grows, and while this is a wonderful benefit in itself, it also means that there are fewer of the opposite sex available who share your level of knowledge and accomplishment.

Equality versus Compatibility

But while intellectual compatibility is a commendable goal in choosing a marriage partner, the challenge is not to define too rigidly what it must mean. The sort of arrangement that makes for healthy intellectual compatibility—the mix of personalities and aptitudes and gifts—in fact varies greatly from relationship to relationship and from marriage to marriage. But to find this arrangement, it will be necessary to let go of the notion that your mate must be your intellectual equal.

God has so constructed us that there are no two individuals on earth who are perfectly equal at any point of potential. Each has certain potentials which the other lacks. The closer you look the greater the differences become. And comparison is always an apples-and-oranges matter.

In addition, it's impossible to predict the direction which individual growth will take in a marriage. Like those who put an unreasonably high premium on sexual attraction, those who insist on an extreme level of intellectual equality with their spouse must set themselves up for disappointment. In time they discover that their personal growth takes place at different speeds, and life takes their creative interests in different directions.

When Evie and I married over sixteen years ago, neither of us had much idea that I would develop a strong interest in writing. Yet today writing is my most enjoyable creative outlet. While Evie enjoys reading my finished product, she has little interest or patience with the ponderous details of making ideas work out on paper, a task which naturally engages all of my creative energy. Evie, on the other hand, has developed an impressive gift for sign language interpretation and communication with the deaf. While I enjoy watching her work, I've not been able to develop the passionate interest in the mechanics of this skill which has spurred her on.

Our situation is typical of most marriages. Creative interests do tend to run in different directions as the years go on. In our case this hasn't been a problem, for we didn't begin marriage with the expectation that all our interests must be identical or that we must maintain some illusive notion of intellectual equality. Marriages where the expectations run high about this are threatened by such diversity.

What, then, should we be looking for in the way of intellectual compatibility with another person? Here the important thing is first to understand what the underlying needs really are that we're hoping will be met through intellectual compatibility—then to look at how well a relationship meets these. First, we hope that marriage will bring mental stimulation to our life. In short, we want the relationship to be *interesting*. Indeed, boredom is perhaps our greatest fear in entering marriage. Secondly, we want the marriage to be an environment where we are encouraged and challenged to realize our full potential, professionally and in other areas. We want our partner to believe in us and spur us on to develop our important gifts. When looked at from this angle, it becomes clear that there are a wide variety of relationship mixes which can fulfill these needs.

Different Models of Intellectual Compatibility
Jerry and Alicia are both teachers in a large city high school; Jerry teaches biology and Alicia teaches chemistry. They met nearly fifteen

years ago when both showed up to help with a student Christian fellowship group that met after school. They were quickly struck with the similarity of their interests in student ministry as well as their common professional and academic goals. They married a year later.

While Jerry and Alicia both greatly enjoy teaching, they find the public school environment stressful, the breakdown in discipline abhorrent, and the work load burdensome. Their mutual involvement in this profession is a continual source of strength and renewal for both of them. The similarity of their subjects, too, allows for frequent interaction on material and lesson plans. They are both strong academics who enjoy long periods of study in their fields. If one wants to spend an evening or a weekend afternoon quietly reading, the other is usually quite amenable and joins in the task. The time often ends with a stimulating discussion of what each has learned.

Jerry and Alicia recognize that even if either should leave the teaching profession, that person would still continue to be an empathetic support to the other. Few would argue that they are intellectually compatible and an enviable match for marriage.

Bill and Ellen are a quite different yet no less impressive example. Now in their late thirties, they've been happily married for over ten years. Ellen is a pediatrician with a successful practice in the suburbs of a Midwestern city. Bill is a physical education instructor working in several local elementary schools. In certain respects Bill and Ellen are as different as day and night. Ellen is drawn to the world of medicine; she thrives on reading medical journals, attending seminars and long evening discussions with professional comrades. Her life revolves around her work, and she strives to stay on the growing edge of her profession. Bill's reading is limited to sports magazines and an occasional novel. While he enjoys discussions about physical fitness, he has no interest in the fine details of medical doctrine. He is, in short, not an academic person. His passion is engaged by competitive sports and the world of outdoor adventure.

In her younger years, until her mid-twenties, Ellen assumed she'd only be happy married to another medical professional. She had two serious relationships, one with a young family physician and one with a surgical intern. Yet as each became more serious she began to worry that the intensity of their common interest in medicine wouldn't make for a healthy marriage. The competitive spirit between them seemed too strong, and there wasn't enough balance of other interests. Also, Ellen longed to raise children and enjoy a reasonably normal family life. It seemed hard to imagine how two physicians addicted to their practices could keep the home fires burning.

Ellen and Bill met at a church social when she was twenty-eight, and he was twenty-seven. Though Ellen instinctively liked Bill, she at first resisted his attempts at a dating relationship, fearing the differences between them were too great. She was won over, however, on a three-day ski trip with singles from their church. Ellen was impressed by Bill's sensitivity to her bungling efforts as a novice skier. He seemed to know exactly what to do to help her gain some skill and confidence in a sport that frankly intimidated her. By the end of the trip she was showing competence on a small slope that surprised even a house instructor.

In the ensuing months Bill introduced Ellen to racquetball and tennis. When she could steal an hour from her practice, she enjoyed going to watch him coach elementary soccer or baseball teams. She was constantly impressed with his ability to motivate these young sports enthusiasts. Evenings with Bill were always enjoyable, too, and Ellen was intrigued with how much fun she had doing simple things with him—attending a movie or going for a milkshake at the Dairy Queen. Though their professional interests were miles apart, they always seemed to have plenty to talk about—dreams of life and family and a mutual interest in community affairs. For the first time Ellen had a relationship which was a diversion from her professional life rather than one which immersed her more in it, and the effect was therapeutic.

Ellen was mildly astonished, too, that Bill was never intimidated by her success or her close friendships with fellow professionals. He wanted her to succeed and realized she needed their support.

Gradually Ellen came to realize that there was the kind of balance in her relationship with Bill that would make for good family life. Ten years of marriage have proven the truth of Ellen's conclusion.

Bill's skill with children has translated well into parenting. He has been an excellent father of their three children, finding time and motivation for parenting which few fathers are able to muster. Ellen has continued to progress in her career, but has welcomed the refuge which family life provides from the stresses of her job. She describes her relationship with Bill as a magnet which pulls her away from her natural obsession with work. Bill has grown in his career as well and was recently offered a principalship.

Balancing Intellectual Compatibility with Other Factors

Bill and Ellen's example brings out two important cautions to keep in mind in weighing intellectual compatibility in a relationship. One is that *balance is as important as similarity.* God not only wants to use a marriage relationship to sharpen our strong points but to strengthen and compensate for our weak points. We need to look carefully not only at how the marriage will do the one but the other as well. The second point is that *we cannot expect our partner to be a savior who provides all of the inspiration for personal growth we will ever need after marriage.* We'll need to continue to draw stimulation from friendships and associations outside of the marriage as well.

Here, to be sure, there are considerable differences in need from individual to individual and from relationship to relationship. Some do best in a situation like Jerry and Alicia's, where similarities seem to outweigh differences. Others, though—especially those who are self-starters by nature—do quite well in an arrangement like Bill and Ellen's. Many others fall somewhere between these extremes.

If you are in your thirties, forties or beyond and have made good strides in your career, you have at least proven one thing: You can grow in your profession without the aid of a marriage relationship. Therefore, you may not need as much intellectual stimulation from marriage as you think. Be open to other options and to how God may wish to complement your life as well as nurture it through marriage and family life.

Again, I'm not saying that intellectual compatibility is unimportant in considering marriage. We simply need to be careful of unreasonable ideals about it and to remember that there are other factors to weigh as well. If you can give a confident affirmative to each of these four questions, then it's reasonable to say that your relationship is intellectually compatible.

1. Do you have enough common areas of interest to keep your relationship interesting? Even though you may have strongly divergent interests in some areas, are there enough common points of interest to give basis to a long-term relationship?

2. Do you have profound respect for each other's gifts and areas of potential? Are you motivated to support and encourage each other at these points, even if your gifts differ considerably? Are you each comfortable with the other having friendships or associations with others who can be a support system for professional or creative growth?

3. Do you each want to be challenged to grow through the other's strong points? Though you will not share every interest in common, are there ways in which you hope the other will challenge you to grow and realize new horizons? Ellen, for instance, benefited immensely from Bill's athletic interests, and Bill was helped by Ellen to better understand some of the medical aspects of sports training. There should be, in other words, some points of contact between your areas of competence and a desire on the part of each of you to benefit from these.

4. Do you communicate well in the areas that will be essential to your life together in marriage? Even though you might be in different worlds professionally or academically, is there good communication and agreement on issues such as lifestyle and family relationships?

Of course when the questions are posed this way, it's not greatly different from asking, "Are you good friends?" In the end *friendship* is the true test of intellectual compatibility.

Does the Husband Have to Be Stronger Intellectually?

An important question remains, however, and that is whether God wills that the husband should always be the clear intellectual superior of the wife in the ideal Christian marriage. Popular Christianity generally assumes so, and many Christians are uncomfortable, in theory at least, with an arrangement like Bill and Ellen's. While the most common question raised to me by Christian men is whether it's O.K. to marry when physical attraction is short of overwhelming, the most common question raised by women is whether they should marry a man whom they perceive is less gifted than they are intellectually or spiritually.

Given the considerable educational advantages which men had throughout biblical times, it can probably be said that the husband was the intellectual superior in most marriages. However, Scripture never says as a matter of principle that the husband must always be intellectually stronger than the wife. To the contrary, in the most extensive description of the characteristics of a good wife, Proverbs 31:10-31, the wife is pictured as more intellectually gifted than the husband at several points: she is a skilled craftsperson (v. 13), astute in business (v. 18), gifted in real estate negotiations (v. 16), a superb manager of domestic affairs (vv. 14-15, 21-22, 27) and a gifted teacher and counselor (v. 26). It is of particular interest that her husband is not threatened by these qualities, but instead praises her (vv. 28-29).

Just as God creates distinctive individuals, so there are distinctive marriages. To say it differently: *there are many different models for a healthy Christian marriage.* While some individuals will only be fulfilled in a traditional arrangement, many women and men are secure enough in themselves and in their relationship with Christ to function quite well in a marriage where the woman is more gifted intellectually, creatively or vocationally.

In many healthy relationships it will simply be impossible to say who is the intellectual superior. Both will have their own gifts, strengths and weaknesses. The wife might have a more glamorous career. Yet the husband, like Bill, may be gifted with athletic or social skills that give him special advantages in parenting. The possibilities and combinations are endless.

In marriages in which the wife clearly has the jump professionally, financially, creatively or intellectually, there will be some concessions to made. The belief that the man should prevail at these points runs deep in our culture and may be a more significant part of your subconscious attitude toward marriage than you realize. You may have to adjust to the fact that your life together will take on a different pattern than you had long imagined would be the case in marriage. The sharing of responsibilities will probably break the conventional mold, and the man will be expected to handle some domestic chores which tradition assigns to the wife. And there may be family members or friends who don't fully accept your arrangement or believe it is a truly Christian model for marriage.

These are all trade-offs, though, that are well worth making, if your motivation for marriage is great enough, your compatibility is strong, and you are entering marriage with your eyes fully open to the concessions that must be made. The important question is not how your relationship meshes with popular ideas of the ideal Christian marriage, but whether it fits God's design of your life and that of your partner. Will it bring out the best in both of you and contribute to your growth in Christ? If so, then you have found a pearl of great price. If gaining this prize means selling off some outmoded expectations, that is not too great a price to pay.

11
Are You
Spiritually
Compatible?

▲▲▲▲▲

Marriages between nonbelievers can be quite happy and successful in many ways. Christians, however, can enjoy fulfillment and fruitfulness in marriage that goes well beyond what others are able to experience. Because of their common bond in Christ they have the potential for marriage that is most uniquely blessed and used by God.

Since spiritual compatibility is essential to this happening, it is in many ways our greatest need in marriage. Yet two cautions must be borne in mind. One is that spiritual compatibility is not a panacea covering all potential problems in marriage. Some Christians do place too much weight on it. It sometimes happens that a couple with a similar spiritual heritage (both from the same church or fellowship, for instance) or a similar commitment to Christian work (both planning to be missionaries) decide to marry without assessing their compatibility in other areas carefully enough. They assume that because both are Christians, conflicts will be transcended and the Lord will take care of all the problems that arise. Yet in time they discover that their differences at certain points are so great as to make life together unbearable.

Here the problem comes in thinking that spiritual compatibility is all that God is concerned about in a relationship. In reality Christ is Lord of the whole life—physical, emotional, social, mental, as well as spiritual. He creates each of us with different needs in these areas and all of these need to be weighed carefully in considering marriage. My purpose in treating spiritual compatibility in the midst of our list rather than at the top of it is to emphasize that it must not be considered in isolation from other areas.

The other caution is that we must be careful not to define spiritual compatibility too narrowly. Christians sometimes equate it too strongly with similarities in spiritual lifestyle, doctrinal belief or Christian vocation. Thus they can be too quick to think they are spiritually compatible with someone who . . .

☐ belongs to the same church, fellowship or denomination

☐ has similar tastes in worship

☐ follows similar devotional practices

☐ is equally knowledgeable about Scripture

☐ has the same spiritual gifts

☐ has similar goals for personal ministry

☐ is equally euphoric about spiritual matters

By the same token they may be too quick to think they are incompatible with someone who doesn't measure up to their expectations at these points. These things, though, often have little to do with whether two people are truly compatible spiritually. We must be careful not to major in minors here. There are certain essentials that are indispensable to a healthy spiritual relationship—points of agreement that must not be lightly brushed over. Beyond these there is much room for diversity on more peripheral matters. How much difference can be tolerated—even enjoyed—depends on the temperamental makeup of the two people. Yet the crucial question is how you agree on the essentials. The rest is often negotiable.

The Essentials of Spiritual Compatibility

What, then, are the essentials of spiritual compatibility in marriage?

1. A common commitment to Christ as Lord and Savior. If Christ has become Lord of your life, it is unthinkable that he would lead you to marry someone without a common dedication to him. Invariably you would find yourself in the untenable position of serving two masters, in conflict over whether to please Christ or your spouse. And you'd deprive yourself for a lifetime of the chance to share the most significant part of your life with your most intimate earthly friend.

Yes, you may win your spouse to Christ. That does happen. Yet in most cases it doesn't. And too often a spouse is tempted to feign an interest in spiritual things simply to please his or her partner. You shouldn't consider marrying someone who hasn't first given their life to Christ in sincerity and then had the opportunity to put down some roots in him.

To this end Scripture commands, "Be ye not unequally yoked together with unbelievers" (2 Cor 6:14 KJV). While scholars argue over whether Paul had marriage in mind in this statement, it is unimaginable that a relationship as binding as marriage wouldn't fall within his boundaries of concern here. The imagery in being unequally yoked is profound and helpful to keep in mind—a horse and ox attached to the same cart and attempting to pull it at different paces is simply not effective.

Even more profoundly, Paul speaks elsewhere of the relationship between husband and wife in terms of the highest analogy he can muster—that of Christ and the church (Eph 5:21-33). The analogy makes little sense if both in the marriage are not Christian. There is a spiritual dimension in marriage which is at the heart of compassion and unity between husband and wife yet only fully possible when both know the Lord.

2. A similar view of biblical authority. Though I'm an evangelical with a firm stand on biblical infallibility, my teaching ministry brings me into many different Christian communions. I recognize that good marriages occur among Christians with a variety of views of biblical authority. The important thing is that husband and wife are reasonably unified in their perspective on this fundamental issue.

The problems that occur when this isn't the case were brought home to me by Jeff and Carolyn, a Christian couple whom I counseled with about two years ago. At first I was impressed by their strong compatibility at important points. Both were adventuresome individuals with a high commitment to social service, and each seemed to have a genuine concern for the other's welfare. Yet Carolyn looked upon the Bible, as I do, as a completely reliable source of God's will for our lives. While Jeff had an admirable respect for Scripture, his view was more liberal and quite tenacious at that; he believed that Scripture should guide our thinking but not be the final authority. The result was that they came out at quite different points on several issues that were important to both of them, and these differences put unfortunate stress on their relationship. As there seemed little hope of reconciling these opinions, I recommended with regret that they shouldn't marry.

What we're speaking of here, of course, is only common sense. Unless you and your partner are working from the same set of instructions, the possibility of conflict is simply too great. Without a unified view of biblical authority, you'll likely find yourselves unequally yoked at more points than would be tolerable in a healthy marriage.

3. A similar understanding of biblical values that are important to family life. Similar views on biblical authority, however, do not guarantee identical interpretations of Scripture. Evangelicals with a high view of Scripture, for instance, come out at different points on the issue of male and female roles in marriage. Whatever your viewpoints on this matter, it's vital that you are in agreement. The question of what priority should be given to family life over church involvement and career is another area where Christians arrive at different points based on different interpretations of Scripture. Again, the important thing is to be of one heart and mind on this central issue.

You and your partner should each be clear about which spiritual and moral values are important to you individually and are nonnegotiable in marriage. You then need to be certain that there is agreement on these points before you go ahead with marriage. Often the help of a third party in sorting this through is beneficial.

4. Extremely important! A desire to continue growing in Christ. As vital as unity is on these key points, it's just as important that each of you desire to continue growing in your relationship with Christ. Without this desire, your spiritual life—individually and together—will stagnate. And without it, sensitivity to differences in each other's perspectives will be hard to come by. The urge for spiritual growth is critical both to personal spiritual health and to the vitality of the relationship.

These four essentials are vital to a healthy Christian marriage and when they are present, differences can often be tolerated, or even enjoyed, at other points of spiritual perspective. It depends greatly on the personalities of the two people. Some will need a high level of similarity at most points related to spiritual life. Others, though, who are secure enough in their relationship with Christ will even thrive and grow through certain differences in spiritual perspective. I've even seen occasional instances where healthy marriages exist with husband and wife attending different churches. Though this isn't normally an ideal arrangement, it shouldn't be categorically ruled out as never acceptable in Christian marriage.

Just recently a Christian woman told me about her own upbringing in a family where the father and mother were active in different denominations. The parents respected each other's positions, yet were open in talking with the children about their differences. She felt strongly that the experience broadened her and her four siblings, making it possible for deeper relationships with Christ.

Male Headship

As with intellectual compatibility, though, we come to the question of male and female roles. What about the traditional view of male headship? Is it necessary for the husband always to be spiritually stronger than the wife and the clear spiritual leader in the relationship? Many Christians would say yes. Yet again we come up against a statistical problem: There are more mature Christian women than men both within the body of Christ as a whole and in most local churches and fellowships. Does this mean that only those women who are fortunate enough to form a bond with a man who is their undisputed spiritual superior are entitled to marry?

Here it is important to understand what Scripture teaches and what it doesn't. Scripture declares that the husband is head of the wife as Christ is head of the church and that the husband is to love his wife as Christ loves the church (Eph 5:23, 25). The wife in turn is to submit herself to her husband as to Christ and to respect her husband (Eph 5:22, 33). Yet Scripture leaves it fairly open as to how the dynamics of this interaction can take place in a given relationship. Again we come back to the fact of different models for a healthy Christian marriage.

Many Christians get locked into certain stereotyped ideas of what male headship must mean in marriage. It's often assumed that the man must have greater spiritual knowledge, be more assertive in matters such as encouraging Bible study, family devotion and church attendance, and in general be a sharper spiritual personality. Yet while some will need these traditional dynamics in their relationship, Scripture doesn't lock us into such stereotypical roles.

God looks more upon the heart than he does upon a person's outward spiritual sharpness or accumulation of spiritual knowledge. I've counseled with several couples considering marriage in which the man simply hasn't had the same advantages for spiritual growth which the woman has had. In one case the woman (Jenny, twenty-nine) belonged to a strong InterVarsity chapter in college and since graduating had been active in a thriving singles ministry of a large, dynamic evangelical church. The man (John, twenty-eight) came to Christ in college through a campus ministry. Then he joined the navy and served in locales where good spiritual nurture simply wasn't available. When I counseled with them, he was stationed at a remote base without a strong church within driving distance.

Jenny had the clear advantages of background here. She was considerably more knowledgeable of Scripture, more comfortable in Christian gatherings and in initiating spiritual matters with John. Yet as I came to know each of them, I felt John's heart for Christ was every bit as strong as Jenny's. He was teachable and was eager to grow. He was supportive of Jenny and not intimidated by her spiritual strength. Because in general he was a mature and congenial individual, and since Jenny strongly respected him, I recommended they marry.

An important part of male headship is supporting the wife at her points of strength. It is commonly thought that male headship means lording it over the wife in spiritual matters. Yet the husband is called to love his wife as Christ loves the church. It must be remembered that Christ's lordship over the church involves a strongly submissive role (Jn 13, for instance, where he washes the disciples' feet), and that Christ loves the church by giving gifts to its members and encouraging them to develop and use them. He even said that his followers in some respects would do greater works than he had done (Jn 14:12).

Part of male headship, then, involves respecting the wife's gifts and encouraging her in their development. In every marriage there is a unique mix of gifts, strengths and weaknesses. In some it will happen that the wife has a stronger gift for spiritual leadership or teaching. If the husband supports and encourages her, and she respects him for his points of strength, it can still be said that the reality of Ephesians 5:21-33 is being worked out. Again, it is of interest that in the six references to Priscilla and Aquila in the New Testament, she is mentioned first in four of them (Acts 18:18, 26; Rom 16:3; 2 Tim 4:19). Apparently she was generally regarded as the stronger individual spiritually.

While Paul uses different spiritual metaphors to depict the role of husband and wife, his overriding concern is that husband and wife be *mutually* submitted to one another. Thus he begins his discussion of husband and wife relations in Ephesians 5 by declaring, "Submit to one another out of reverence for Christ" (a verse that is often omitted in traditional discussions of male/female roles!). In 1 Corinthians 7:4 he makes the same point regarding the physical relationship in marriage: "The wife's body does not belong to her alone but also to her husband. In the same way, the husband's body does not belong to him alone but also to his wife." The notion of mutual submission implies that either husband or wife may have an authority role at different points in the marriage. Paul is clearly not suggesting a rigid pattern of hierarchy but a situation where there will be a lot of give and take.

Beyond Male Headship

While many Christians follow a straightforward interpretation of Paul's teachings, an increasing number of believers with a high view of biblical authority have concluded that headship was not meant to be binding for Christians of all times.[1] It is thought that this was intended to correct some unfortunate circumstances in the early churches or as an acquiescence to the culture of that time. Wives were told to submit to their husbands so that Christians would not challenge a social custom in a way that would hinder the spread of the gospel. In the same way Christian women were instructed to wear veils and not to talk during worship.

These commands, it is argued, should be seen in the same class as those about slaves obeying their masters. They had their place in the culture of the first century. But just as we would no longer look upon slavery as God's perfect will, neither should we insist on male head-ship in marriage as God's idea. God's highest design for marriage is reflected in Galatians 3:28, where Paul says, "There is neither Jew nor Greek, slave nor free, male nor female, for you are all one in Christ Jesus." The unity portrayed in that passage should be understood as touching all aspects of life, not simply the spiritual, and has important bearing on the marriage relationship.

If you believe that Paul's commands on male/female roles in mar-riage were culturally conditioned, then of course you will not feel constrained to follow the traditional rule of the husband being the stronger spiritual personality in marriage. You will understand the New Testament as allowing latitude on this matter, while still encour-aging mutual respect, love and spiritual maturity within the marriage relationship. But even the straightforward reading of Paul's teachings brings us to the same conclusion once the full breadth of his thinking is understood.

Paul seems much more intent on encouraging mutual submission and partnership in marriage than a rigid spiritual role pattern. In the end, whichever interpretive approach you take to Scripture you come out at virtually the same point—that there are different possibilities for the spiritual maturity mix between husband and wife. The vital matter is that each be intent upon following and growing in Christ and upon being a redemptive spiritual companion to the other.

12
Are You
Emotionally
Compatible?

▲▬▲▬▲▬▲▬▲

W hen Nathan and Cecilia married, they had high hopes of working together in ministry. With Nathan's seminary training and Cecilia's experience in church education, they seemed an ideal match. They married shortly after Nathan graduated and immediately accepted a call to pastor a fledgling church in New England.

After four years under their leadership, the church had grown from fewer than fifty members to over two hundred. Cecilia and Nathan were well accepted and loved by these people, and both worked tirelessly. Enthusiasm ran high in this young flock, which already was taking steps toward building its first facility on a piece of land donated by a generous member.

Given these factors, Cecilia was astonished when Nathan suggested they consider accepting an offer to begin a new church in Kansas City. She couldn't imagine quitting a situation that was going so well, and the thought of leaving these people who depended on them so greatly smacked of desertion. Nathan was equally astonished that Cecilia couldn't understand his enthusiasm for this new adventure. And far from thinking of leaving as desertion, Nathan felt their present church would benefit from fresh blood. "We've done our job here," he insisted. "We've gotten the fire burning, but it's time for someone else to come in and fan the flame."

For several weeks the issue brought them to an impasse whenever it came up, and tension mounted. Finally they agreed to meet with a denominational counselor and let him advise them what to do. After three sessions, the counselor concluded: "I simply cannot tell you which direction to go. Both are equally justified. What you're dealing with here is a fundamental difference in personality. Nathan by his very nature is motivated to seek variety and new adventure. Cecilia has a need to nurture situations that are already successful. You'll do best to honestly face your differences and seek a compromise."

Distinctive Motivations

Nathan and Cecilia's example brings us to the heart of another compatibility issue which we need to look at—*emotional compatibility*. We're reminded of the sorts of conflicts that can occur when two people are motivated in basically different ways.

Scripture attests that God fashions each of our lives with a unique motivational pattern. The result is that our natural emotional responses to the events of life are different. We each instinctively enjoy certain types of activities and incline toward certain tastes. Our personal judgments, too, of what is best for us and even of more fundamental questions of right and wrong are strongly affected by this motivational pattern. This motivational pattern is at the heart of what is meant by personality, or our unique psychological orientation to life.[1]

The idea that God gives distinctive personality is not well accepted by all believers. Many equate personality with the old nature which has been erased by Christ. Scripture, though, never comes close to such a spiritualized concept of personality. To the contrary, Psalm 139:13 declares that God creates our "inward parts," a term used by the Hebrews to signify the personality or distinctive emotional life of a person.[2] Paul, too, speaks to this idea in 1 Corinthians 12:4-6, where he notes that God endows each of us with distinctive *working*, which in the Greek means "energizing" or "motivation."

What does the New Testament mean, then, when it says that we who have been born of Christ have a new nature? It is crucial to understand that when the New Testament speaks of our new nature in Christ, it is not referring to the annulment of our personalities, but the redirection of them. The two natures refer to different allegiances for our personality. Under the old nature I resist God's will, while under the new nature I joyfully respond to it. Yet it is still my own unique personality which responds in either case. Thus we find hundreds of examples throughout Scripture of individuals doing the will of God from their hearts but in their own highly distinctive ways. Our individual personalities are the stamp of God's image upon us.[3]

The Significance of Personality in Choosing a Mate

Each of us will do well to take what steps we can to understand our personality. There are few areas where the ancient adage "know thyself" more clearly applies. Through understanding the motivational tendencies that are most fundamental to our being, we gain a treasured insight not only into how God has designed our life but into what he wants us to do with it.

Having said that, it must also be said that we can exaggerate the significance of the personality factor in choosing a mate. The idea of matching personality types has become quite faddish during the last decade and a near obsession in some circles. Pop theories abound, promising to unfold the hidden mysteries of your personality through analysis of some single factor (everything from blood types to birth order to "colors" of your personality to signs in the Zodiac is claimed to hold the key). Then they will tell you with prophetic certainty what personality type you must match with to assure a happy marriage. Each theory contends that certain personality combinations are destined for success in marriage, others for failure.

A simple look around you, though, reveals the lie in this extreme notion. You don't have to look far to find examples of virtually every combination of personalities imaginable existing together in happy marriages. It's not hard, either, to find examples of couples who seem well-matched personality wise, yet have not done well in marriage. Common sense tells us that personality doesn't hold some mystical key to success or failure in marriage.

The fact is that there are inherent strengths and weaknesses to any combination of two personalities in a marriage relationship. Any mix of personality types can work well in marriage if both individuals are mature and compatible at other points. Likewise, any combination, even the most seemingly compatible, can be disastrous if other factors don't line up well.

There is considerable benefit to understanding each other's personalities, to be sure. But the value comes in helping you understand where your potential for conflict will lie rather than in giving you a magical answer about whether or not to marry. It shouldn't be thought that personality is some esoteric factor beyond others we're looking at which might annul or confirm a decision to marry.

Nathan and Cecilia's conflict, for instance, didn't prove that their personalities were poorly matched for marriage. In fact these two were highly compatible. What their conflict revealed was that they didn't understand their personality differences well enough. They should have gone into marriage with a clearer understanding of their different motivational patterns. As they came to appreciate these differences, they were quite willing to make adjustments, and this is what compatibility is all about. (Their solution: Stay another year at the New

England church, then look for a new opportunity; commit themselves to a five-year term with any church they serve in the future.)

My advice to couples considering marriage is first to weigh the other compatibility factors we're looking at. Do you feel strong compassion for each other? Is your friendship strong? Is the sexual attraction strong enough to justify marriage? Are you intellectually and spiritually compatible in ways that are important to both of you? Then look carefully at how your expectations match at important points (discussed in the next chapter). Finally, carefully consider whether you are both ready for a lifetime commitment. Do you have good evidence to support your conclusion?

At this point you should have sufficient information to make a wise and confident decision about marriage. If you choose to marry, then look more closely at your personality differences. Take a test or work through an exercise together. Talk about the results or discuss them with a professional counselor or trusted friend. Note where the strengths and weaknesses in your relationship lie. Look carefully at where adjustments and compromises will be needed.

But determine in advance that you will be willing to make these adjustments, even before you know what they must be. If you care deeply for the other person and are mature enough for marriage, you will be willing to. Don't let the results of personality analysis, which are always highly subjective and never completely reliable, deter you from going ahead with marriage if you are otherwise convinced that you should—or convince you to marry if you are otherwise uncertain. Simply take these results as a further help toward entering marriage with your eyes open.

Understanding Each Other's Motivational Pattern
What are specific steps you can take to better understand your personalities? Any standardized personality test, offered through a church, counseling service or college vocational center can serve the purpose, provided you both take the same test and have competent

instruction on interpreting the results. In my own area, Washington D. C., Fourth Presbyterian Church offers personality testing for those planning to marry and then provides counseling on the results. I'm sure that if you ask around you'll find other large churches offering the same service.

If you prefer to do this without outside help, let me suggest a simple and enjoyable exercise.[4] Pick a quiet setting and a time when you are both relaxed and free from other pressures. First, decide together upon a method for classifying personalities. If you are not already familiar with a particular approach, you can use the traditional Hippocratic model. While limited, it does provide a track to run on and makes for good discussion. With all of its limitations, Christian psychiatrist Paul Tournier insists that this "classification . . . is still the best. Proof of this is that with only minor variations numerous authors make what is basically the same classifications into types."[5] It recognizes four prominent personality types:

☐ The *choleric*—inclined toward action, leadership, change, getting things done.

☐ The *sanguine*—inclined toward feeling, empathy.

☐ The *melancholic*—inclined toward thinking, analysis.

☐ The *phlegmatic*—inclined toward maintaining order, accepting things as they are.[6]

Be certain that both of you are in clear agreement about what these terms mean.

Then spend thirty minutes silently reflecting on your lives, with pen and paper handy to write down your thoughts. Try to identify the experiences that have been most successful or meaningful to you, from early childhood to the present. Think of this as an ink-blot test—your first impressions count the most. Write a one-sentence description of each important accomplishment that comes to mind. Note the experiences that were important to you, whether or not you think anyone else was impressed with them. What comes to mind may be anything from running a successful lemonade stand when you were five to passing algebra in eighth grade to getting your Ph.D. at thirty. Try to come up with twenty to thirty examples each.

When you finish, give your lists to each other. Then allow fifteen minutes for each to reflect silently on the other's responses. Regard these responses as a map to your partner's motivational pattern. Try to determine what the most basic personality characteristic is that underlies the accomplishments that he or she has listed as important. Do they seem to indicate a desire to lead, for instance (choleric)? To probe for deeper understanding (melancholic)? To enjoy life (sanguine)? To make life more orderly (phlegmatic)? Finally, drawing on your conclusion and on all other knowledge that you have of your partner, list the personality categories in the order that you think best describes her or him (choleric-phlegmatic-sanguine-melancholic, for instance). Then share your conclusions with each other.

Of course, allow the other a fair hearing if he or she thinks your description is inaccurate. Listen carefully to the reasons and if necessary revise your description. But realize that if your opinions vary widely, the truth probably lies somewhere between the extremes.

Finally, accept your descriptions of each other as, while imperfect, at least a track to run on and a basis for discussing the dynamics of your relationship in marriage. Look honestly at where the strengths and weaknesses in your relationship are likely to lie. Note especially how the dominant thrusts in your personalities are likely to influence the way you respond to life and to each other.

How Different Personalities Interact

While you probably won't find it difficult to identify strengths and weaknesses in your personality mix, once your individual motivational patterns are understood, some examples of how the classic personality types interact may help. Again, I draw on these for the sake of simplicity, realizing that no one perfectly matches any of these ideal types.

A relationship between two cholerics produces a marriage with very strong leadership potential. If there is agreement between you on your goals, you'll stoke each other's fire considerably and be a great service to those whom you work with. Yet the potential for butting heads in this combination is also great. Considerable compassion and patience with each other will be needed.

When the choleric personality combines with any other type, the choleric brings leadership and motivational strength to the relationship. The choleric can inspire the sanguine, melancholic or phlegmatic to set goals and to break the inertia tendencies to which each of these types is vulnerable. Likewise, each of these can have a redemptive influence on the choleric. The sanguine can deepen the feeling capacity of the choleric; the melancholic can help the choleric to approach life more thoughtfully, and the phlegmatic can inspire needed patience, caution and organizational skills. Yet the choleric can be impatient with the changeable emotions of the sanguine, the analytical spirit of the melancholic or the meticulousness of the phlegmatic. Likewise, each of these can be intolerant of the choleric's high energy approach to life and the obsession with achievement and goals.

A sanguine-sanguine combination can produce a highly empathetic marriage, one that is capable of showing great compassion toward children and others. The danger in this combination is lack of discipline, as sanguines tend to get caught up in the emotions of the moment.

In a sanguine-melancholic relationship, the empathetic sanguine can give needed emotional support to the melancholic's probing concerns. The sanguine can also help the melancholic more to enjoy the moment and to break out of moodiness. The latter can help the sanguine to think as well as feel, to get beyond the grip of immediate feelings, and to see different sides of issues which the sanguine may tend to judge too quickly by instinct alone. The danger in this mix, again, can be impatience—the sanguine with the ponderousness of the melancholic, the latter with the changeability of the sanguine. Also, sanguines, with their highly empathetic nature, can get drawn into the melancholic's moodiness yet not be able to handle that state as well or derive the creative benefit from it which the melancholic often does.

In a sanguine-phlegmatic marriage, the phlegmatic can bring discipline and order to the sanguine's potentially chaotic life, while the sanguine can help the phlegmatic to better recognize and experience feelings. Again, as in other mixes, patience and acceptance can be a challenge. The sanguine may regard the phlegmatic as too mechanical and chide the phlegmatic for being out of touch with feelings, while the latter may view the sanguine as fickle or capricious.

The obvious danger of a melancholic-melancholic relationship is moodiness and depression. Two melancholics may drag each other into such an analytical spirit that the practicalities of life are ignored. Yet important artistic and intellectual achievements are sometimes born out of such relationships, and two melancholics can have a knack for inspiring each other to greater horizons. The arrangement can work well among two mature individuals.

A melancholic-phlegmatic arrangement can be excellent if each is accepting and respectful of the other's special gifts. The phlegmatic can help the melancholic to achieve the personal organization that is so important to achieving his or her creative goals. The melancholic in turn can deepen the phlegmatic. Again, the potential for impatience and intolerance of each other's inclinations is obvious.

Finally, the phlegmatic-phlegmatic mix is of all the combinations the one least prone to conflict, for phlegmatics tend by nature to be more stoic and to enjoy the endless range of routine details necessary to maintaining a home and family life. Dangers in this arrangement include boredom and insensitivity to the temperamental distinctions of children.

Each of these combinations brings out the fact that while there is beauty and special potential in any mix of two personalities, there are vulnerabilities and potential problems as well. Any of these combinations can work well among mature, compassionate individuals. Again, we are reminded that marriage is for adults—for those who regard their differences not as a threat but an inspiration for growth, who are determined to negotiate their differences and who ultimately view the relationship as more important than their own individuality.

We are reminded, too, of the need for each having friendships and associations outside of the marriage which inspire strength and growth at points where the marriage relationship is weak or vulnerable. While marriage is the most important human relationship we enter into, it can never be expected to meet all of our growth or companionship needs.

13
Are Your
Expectations
Compatible?

▲ ▲ ▲ ▲ ▲

One Sunday evening after church, when I was a young Christian, I asked some friends to go with me to see an old musician friend perform in Waldorf, Maryland, about an hour's drive away. The place we were headed for was, to put it politely, a dive, and I assumed the others knew this.

A woman in the group asked if she could first stop by home to change her clothes. We dropped her off, then waited for her in the car for some time. Finally she emerged dressed fit to kill.

On the way someone finally mustered the courage to ask her why she was so finely dressed for the sort of establishment we were going to visit. Didn't she know there were no plush clubs in Waldorf? Astonished, she replied, "I thought you said we were going to *the* Waldorf."[1]

The incident is a classic example of how false expectations arise. In this case I assumed that my friend knew exactly where we were going, while she of course drew a quite different conclusion from what I said.

On a much more serious level, the problem of differing expectations is a real one for two people entering marriage. All too often each person carries quite different assumptions about what life together will be like. Even when there is no attempt to deceive, each may develop certain expectations which are not understood or shared by the other. One may be expecting the Waldorf, while the other has a quite different idea in mind.

For this reason, it is extremely important that two people considering marriage spend considerable time discussing and comparing their expectations and looking honestly at how these are likely to mesh. While we have already looked at some of the most important areas, there are a number of other areas of perspective on lifestyle and family life in which unity or flexibility is essential. As we've seen, congeniality and flexibility are vital factors in marriage. Yet even the most flexible person brings to marriage certain expectations which are inseparable from his or her idea of a successful marriage. I hope this chapter will challenge you to look carefully at how well your expectations match in areas that are important to you.

Significant Areas of Expectation

Male and female roles. Regardless of where you come out on the issue of male headship, there are still many practical questions about male and female roles that you will need to resolve. In *How to Choose the Wrong Marriage Partner and Live Unhappily Ever After*, Robert Mason and Caroline Jacobs list conflict over roles first among twenty-eight factors likely to deteriorate a marriage.[1] I agree, as this has been a major factor in the majority of Christian marriage breakups which I've witnessed.

I find that most often when there is conflict over male and female roles in a Christian marriage, the man entered marriage expecting a fairly traditional arrangement while the woman wanted greater freedom. Yet even couples who believe in equal partnership face many practical role questions which can cause conflict.

Is the wife expected to work? If so, does she have the same freedom to pursue a career as the husband does? If children come along, will either be expected to cut back their work hours or in other ways carry greater responsibility for parenting? Who'll get up at 3:00 A.M. to change the diaper? And what about the endless range of domestic responsibilities—such as, cooking, cleaning, maintaining the home and yard, paying bills and preparing to entertain guests? How will the burdens be divided?

My purpose is not to recommend one perspective on male and female roles over another. Again, there are many workable models for a good marriage. The important matter is to agree on what the arrangement will be.

Educational goals. Frequently it's expected that one spouse will work to give the other the benefit of finishing college or grad school. If so, is the other expected to return the favor once his or her program is completed? Be sure to have clear agreement on this question before marrying, for the potential for misunderstanding and hurt feelings here is great.

Standard of living. It's often argued that one should only marry someone from his or her same economic background. A woman who has grown up in a large home in the suburbs will not do well with a man from the inner city, for instance.

In reality, marriages between those of different economic backgrounds sometimes work well, and of course marriages between those of similar backgrounds sometimes fizzle. Here expectations play a much greater role than past experience. A man from a poor family might have a perfectly happy marriage with a woman raised in Beverly

Hills if they both have similar expectations for their lifestyle. By the same token, two people from similar backgrounds may have radically different aspirations for their future.

Of course flexibility about your economic future is essential. You can never predict how the financial tide will turn. Yet unless there is reasonable agreement between you about the standard of living you would like to achieve, the potential for conflict will be considerable.

While it is important to talk about your desires for your standard of living, it is just as important to be clear about your values. Are there moral, spiritual or ministry considerations which affect the way you think about your economic future? Don't assume that because both of you are Christians you will automatically be of one mind on this issue.

Some Christians believe as a matter of principle that they should keep their lifestyle as simple as possible, others that their standard of living should have a clearly defined upper limit, while others insist that you shouldn't place limits on the blessings God may bestow on you. Christians vary, too, on the question of giving. How much of your income will you plan to tithe? And what types of concerns will you give to?

Be sure that you have a clear understanding of each other's "wants" and "oughts." This is an area where your desires and values need to be in close agreement.

Vocational goals. Beyond questions of male and female roles, does either of you have a vocational goal which would affect family life in a way that would be unacceptable to the other? The man who wants to be a pastor will have a difficult marriage with a woman who puts a high premium on family privacy. The woman who wants to be a physician will need a husband who is highly tolerant of the erratic lifestyle involved.

Christians sometimes ask me whether the opportunity for marriage should ever be a reason for reconsidering your vocational goals. Suppose, for instance, that you've been planning to become a missionary but now have the opportunity to marry someone who isn't open to missionary service or to living in a different culture? Would you be selling out to change your career plans for the sake of marrying this person? (While this question is most frequently asked me by those entering missionary or ministry-related vocations, it's sometimes raised by others as well.)

My answer is that it depends upon the reasons underlying your career choice. Does this vocation seem to fit your gifts and your motivational pattern better than any other? Then you should only consider marrying someone who can be supportive of your vocational goals. If, however, you are less than certain about where your strongest gifts and motivations lie, you should feel free to stay flexible about your career direction. God could use the opportunity for marriage as much as any other circumstance to lead you. Unfortunately, our Christian culture does not make it easy for you at this point. Some Christian groups place a high priority upon first resolving your vocational choice, then choosing a mate. If the one you want to marry is not open to your vocational goals, then find someone else ("Master, mission, mate," as the adage goes).

Scripture, though, never constrains us to such a rigid chronology in life's choices. When we consider the very high priority Paul places upon those who want to marry doing so when the opportunity is present (1 Cor 7), we must conclude that there are times when the choice of a mate should precede the choice of a vocation. It will vary from person to person, but we are not locked into an inflexible pattern.

We hear so much talk, too, about God giving believers a "call" to a vocation which they are locked into forever. Many assume that once they feel a strong inspiration to follow a certain vocation, from that point on they are not free to reconsider. However, such a moment of inspiration is usually a psychological experience giving you insight into your deepest desires and not a direct and binding message from God.[2] It is used by him to help you understand what you most want to do at the time, but it should not be taken as a permanent mandate. Your experience of inspiration is based upon your own understanding at that point—of yourself, of God, of opportunities in the world. As your understanding grows and changes, your sense of inspiration about what to do with your life may change also.

When we carefully examine Scripture on the point, we find that most of the time God guides not through a blinding revelation which tells you once and for all what he wants you to do for the rest of your life but incrementally, each day bringing new insight into his plan for your life. The opportunity for marriage can be as much a part of this process of enlightenment as anything.

In any case, you shouldn't feel guilty for rethinking your career plans. You may or may not decide that the opportunity for marriage is a reason to change them. But you should at least feel free to consider the possibility.

Number of children and timing. Many entering marriage are quite happy to stay open on this question and let time and circumstance decide the family constellation. Others, though, have strong feelings about wanting a family of a certain size. And some are not eager to have children. Few issues are more important to talk through before marriage.

Relationship to in-laws. Will an in-law live with you? How much involvement with the spouse's family is expected? Expectations on this level can differ widely and be a considerable source of contention.

Social expectations. How public or private will your life together be? Does either of you feel strongly that you must be involved together as a couple in certain social activities, groups or relationships?

Time together. How much premium do you each put on planned, private time together? Does either have a strong need for frequent, regular time set aside for being together alone as a couple?

Geographic expectations. Will you or your partner only be happy living in a certain geographical region or in a certain type of area—urban, country, suburban, ethnic, and so on?

Recreational desires and hobbies. Again, this is an area where many couples are highly flexible. But some do feel strongly that they and their spouse should be involved together in certain recreational activities. Don't take it for granted that you both agree about this.

Make Your Own List

While these are some of the areas of expectation where flexibility or mutuality is most essential in marriage, the ones I've suggested have been partly to prime the pump. You can undoubtedly think of others that will be significant to your own marriage. I would, in fact, strongly encourage you each to make a list of all the important expectations that you hold for marriage. If you find that either of you has a strong expectation which isn't shared by the other and isn't negotiable, I would advise you not to marry unless this difference can be reconciled.

On the other hand, if your expectations align well at these points— or are truly flexible—you have another excellent indication of compatibility. If your relationship measures well in the other areas we've looked at, this is the final green light you need to make a confident decision to marry.

14
Finally
Deciding

▲▲▲▲▲

I f you are in a serious relationship and have been trying to decide whether to marry as you read, it's possible you have already reached a decision. It may be that a single issue was holding you back, and it no longer seems so crucial. Or it may be that exploring the compatibility factors has enabled you to resolve the direction of your relationship.

Yet it's possible, too, that you are still on the fence about what to do. You may be fairly certain about marrying but not convinced enough to make a firm decision. This could mean that you need to allow more time for getting to know one another better. But it's also possible that you already do know everything you need to know—or are likely to be able to discover—to make a responsible decision about whether to marry. This is probably true if all of the following applies:

☐ You and your partner are both at least twenty-five years old.

☐ Your relationship is already well into its second year, or beyond.

☐ You have spent considerable time together during this period. In other words, this hasn't been a long-distance relationship; you've been together frequently and under a wide variety of circumstances.

☐ Your communication has been good.

☐ You have carefully weighed your compatibility at the important points, and you match up well. You are both mature enough for marriage. There are no major red flags.

☐ There is no significant extenuating circumstance yet to be resolved (such as career direction or a decision about education) which could have bearing on whether you decide to marry.

If you meet these criteria, then chances are good you are at a point where you can make a responsible decision about marriage. If you doubt you are actually there yet, then consider the following:

☐ What additional information could you gain that would allow you to make this decision with greater confidence?

☐ By waiting longer will you be in a better position to make an informed decision? Why?

☐ What else might be gained by delaying the decision?

If you are not able to give a good answer to any of these questions, then it's probable you already are in a position to make a responsible decision.

This isn't to say that you should feel compelled to decide at this time. If both of you are comfortable letting the relationship continue undefined, then of course you should feel free to stay uncommitted. Yet if your partner is convinced about marriage and eager to go ahead, then you may owe it to him or her to take steps to try to resolve your own feelings. This is particularly true if you're already at least fairly convinced, yet still feel the need for some final confirmation.

If this is your situation, then there are two steps which I highly recommend that you take.

Getting Counsel

First, select at least three people whom you respect and ask them if they will meet with you to advise you about your decision. Though a group meeting can have its advantages, you will probably do best to meet separately with each person. At least two of these advisors should be married individuals with some years in an established happy marriage, and of course it's fine to meet with a couple. If you have a good relationship with your own parents, include them. Including your pastor or a professional counselor is often a good idea as well.

Request specifically to meet with each person for an hour, and select an unhurried time and a setting where you're not likely to be interrupted. When you meet, give the person some background on your relationship (if he or she is not already familiar with it) and explain what you see to be the pros and cons of marrying. Ask them to tell you if they see further issues you should consider. Then ask them, if they are willing, to venture their opinion on whether you should marry or not.

One reason you may resist doing this is because you fear that others won't really want to help you. You feel that you're intruding on their time, and if they agree to meet with you, it will only be reluctantly. Let me assure you that most people greatly enjoy giving advice and are flattered to be asked for it, particularly with a decision as important as marriage. I think you'll find most not only willing, but quite happy to talk with you. Even very busy pastors find it refreshing to deal with an issue as enjoyable as marriage in the midst of the more distressing concerns that often absorb their time. (My only advice is to be specific about requesting an hour and don't let the meeting drag on beyond this. If the other person wants to extend it, fine, but let him or her take the initiative.)

Another reason you may hesitate to seek counsel is the fear that others will spiritualize the issues and not deal directly with your concerns. You may fear getting a response like, "Don't worry, you'll have perfect peace when it's time to go ahead." Or "Just let the Lord show you in his own way and time what to do." You may even fear that they will make you feel silly for approaching the marriage decision as an issue, rather than simply waiting for clear spiritual guidance.

If you do unwittingly end up with persons who spiritualize, graciously thank them for their insight—for they may be responding from the most compassionate and reverent motives—but move on and look for someone who is willing to address the issues more directly. Above all, don't let one who spiritualizes lay a guilt trip on you for taking a more practical approach to your decision. You are being every bit as spiritual as they are. You are simply seeking to obey the Lord's command to use the mind he has given you for making responsible decisions.

There are many people who will give you a thoughtful and sensitive response. They will readily appreciate the issues you're wrestling with and be more than happy to talk them through with you. The key is to be careful whom you choose to counsel you.

In terms of evaluating the advice you receive, you should resist the temptation to think that any person is giving you the final answer about what to do. It is particularly tempting to think this if he or she is a spiritual authority whom you highly revere, a parent or someone with a strong personality. Yet while you should respect their counsel and weigh it carefully, you should take the counsel as *advice,* not prophecy. Remember that the value of counsel in the biblical understanding is not to give you a crystal ball insight into God's will, but to stimulate your thinking—to stretch you to think more deeply and clearly about an issue, to see new alternatives and old ones in a new light. In the end it remains your responsibility before God to make your own decision. Even if what you decide to do differs from what anyone has advised, you have still benefited greatly from the process of getting counsel.

Of course, if all of your counselors advise you to do the same thing (to marry or not to marry), then there's a good possibility this is the course you should follow. The burden of proof is more strongly upon you now to show why you shouldn't go this direction. Yet sometimes the burden of proof can be met, and Scripture is full of examples where one person was right against the multitude. The important thing is to have a clear reason for what you decide. Clear-minded thinking should be your goal. Usually, getting advice from a multitude (or at least a small multitude) of counselors will help you greatly toward this end.

Taking a Personal Retreat

After you have talked your decision through with at least several people, I recommend that you take a personal retreat. My conviction about the value of doing this springs from my own experience as much as anything. It was on a one-and-a-half-day silent retreat in the winter of 1973 that I first realized that I really did want to marry Evie. It took some uncluttered time for me to sort this through, and the return on that very small investment of time has been indescribable.

By "personal retreat" I mean a period of time set aside for being alone with the Lord to pray and think through your decision. I recommend investing at least one full day in which you are by yourself from the time you get up in the morning until when you go to bed. If you can manage a full weekend or several days for this, then do it.

I find that most Christians have never taken even a one-day personal retreat. They resist the thought of spending this much time alone, setting other responsibilities aside in order to do it. My question is, can you afford *not* to do it? Next to your decision to follow Christ, you are facing the most important choice of your life in your decision about marriage.

You should choose a pleasant, reflective environment for this getaway. It should be away from normal distractions and a place where you will not expect to be interrupted. A regional, state or national park can provide an excellent and inexpensive setting, depending upon weather and seasonal factors. A motel room, especially at a beach or vacation resort, can work quite well also. A superb alternative, if available in your area, is a Christian retreat center. Many conference centers which cater to groups also make provision for individual and silent retreats. Often, too, the cost is much less than a commercial motel room.

It's important to know something about the place you will visit. Will the setting be quiet? Will you have a room to yourself that is large enough for your needs? Are there other events going on at the center which would be distracting? You wouldn't want to count on doing much meditation in a camp where a major youth conference is being held!

Be sure to make allowance for your food needs. If you're going to a retreat center, find out if meals will be available. If not, or if you're going to a park, bring enough food with you. If you're going to a motel, be sure it's in an area where restaurants are accessible. Of course, you can plan to fast during this time. But if you're not accustomed to fasting, this shouldn't be the occasion to make your first try.

If you're going to a retreat center, it's also important to know that the room will be adequately heated. If it sounds like I'm being too picky about details, I can only tell you that from much experience with personal retreats, it's the little foxes that spoil the vines. Satan will find any way he can to interfere with a time set aside for meditation, and he uses minor irritations quite as effectively as major ones. Careful planning is essential, to be certain the situational factors will contribute as much as possible to a positive experience.

What to Do on Your Personal Retreat

I recommend beginning your retreat time with some Scripture reading, to focus your mind on God's grace and sufficiency. Picking several psalms at random and reading them slowly and reflectively is an excellent idea. Follow this with a time of prayer, preferably at least an hour. Spend at least half of that time thanking God for his past provision in your life.

Focus especially on relationships, particularly on the one you have come to pray about. Thank him for bringing the two of you together and for as many positive factors in the relationship as you can think of. Thank him also for the challenges you've experienced in the relationship and for any other aspects of the relationship that come to mind. Thank him, too, for the confidence you can have about the future—the knowledge that he will protect you and guide you within a plan that reflects his very best for you.

Then pray that he will guide your decision about marriage and give you the mind of Christ in making it. Ask, too, that he will give you the strength to do his will and to take the steps of faith that will be involved. Ask him to give balance to your thinking—to keep you from being either unreasonably idealistic or too quick to compromise. Ask him to work out his very best in your life and your partner's.

Spend the remaining time on this personal retreat reflecting on your relationship and its future, thinking through the possibility of marriage as thoroughly as you can. It may be helpful to take this book along with you and to reread section three in order to identify the issues you need to be concerned with as clearly as possible. Carefully consider your relationship, noting the positive and negative factors. You may find it beneficial to write down your thoughts. Try listing in columns the pros and cons of going ahead with marriage. Then, reflecting on this list, consider which direction seems to be more appropriate.

As the day (or the time) moves on, note carefully if one impression about what to do seems to be stronger than the others. Do you lean toward marriage, away from it or toward waiting for further insight? Don't look for perfect certainty—a psychological impossibility for most of us—but for *substantial* assurance about which direction to go. If you feel reasonably assured that you should marry, I would take that impression as reliable at this point. This is the point where you are justified in taking a step of faith. Go ahead and resolve to marry. If perchance you've made the wrong choice, trust that God will make that clear to you in the days ahead.

If your assurance is not strong enough to do this, then of course you shouldn't push yourself to a decision but should decide to wait for further insight. If you feel strongly that marriage is not recommended, then you should decide not to marry and be honest in sharing that with your partner. Pray that God will give you the compassion and sensitivity to share this conclusion with him or her.

Whatever you resolve to do during this time, you should close your personal retreat with another period of prayer, thanking God for his guidance during the time and requesting his continued direction in your relationship. Ask him to redirect any unjustified conclusions you have reached and to overrule any wrong decision you might have made.

Keeping Your Head

During a time of personal reflection, you may experience a strong inspiration about what direction to follow. It's very easy to think that this inspiration is a direct revelation from God, little short of an audible voice telling you what to do. In reality, it's normally a psychological experience, not God revealing himself. You're discovering what it is underneath that you really want to do or think you ought to do. This insight is extremely important in understanding what God wills for you. If you have committed your meditation time to God and asked him to lead your thoughts, you can trust that the conclusion you've reached is guided by him. It is indicative of what he wants you to plan on doing at this time.

I choose my words carefully for this is something short of saying that God has *directly revealed* to you what to do. If you think the latter, you'll be inclined to believe that God has laid an irreversible mandate on you to marry, giving you a revelation about the future. In reality your understanding of his will at this point is only as good as the information to which you've been exposed. It's possible that unexpected new information could suggest the need to change your decision. You at least need to stay open to this possibility, even after making a firm decision to marry, up until the time you finally take your vows.

I don't mean to imply that this will be likely. It's unlikely now that you will make some radically new discovery that will suggest revising your decision to marry. Yet none of us knows the future and that possibility can never be discounted. This again throws us into the realm of walking by faith at each point of our journey toward marriage.

There is another side to this which is just as important to emphasize. Even if you become firmly convinced during a personal retreat that you should marry, you will probably have some apprehensions between then and when you finally walk the aisle. Some second thoughts will be normal. Unless there is some overriding and obvious reason why you should rethink your choice, though, you should hold firm to your decision to marry. If your mood swings are so great that you feel compelled to call off the engagement, and if there is no strong and clear reason for doing so, you should look carefully at whether an underlying fear of commitment is keeping you from being able to stay the course toward marriage.

Again, though, remember that some fear and doubt in the face of a step as enormous as marriage is very normal. Look for substantial certainty, not perfect assurance, then go ahead in that confidence, even if some apprehensions recur.

IV
Finding
a
Spouse

15
What Will
Attract Someone
to You?

▲ ▲ ▲ ▲ ▲

Among the happily married people whom I know is a woman who suffered severe disfiguration in a tragic burn accident when she was twenty. Few gave her hope for living a normal life after that. Yet after a long convalescence, Shelly, who had a remarkable faith in Christ, took a positive approach to life. She found a secretarial job in which she was able to compensate in impressive ways for her loss of functions. She became active in a large Christian singles group. She gave close attention to her personal appearance, proving that she could be attractive in spite of her limitations. In time she had several dating relationships, and later married.

Shelly's is only one of many examples I could mention of persons who have found excellent marriages in spite of factors that would have discouraged others from even trying. I talk with many Christians who are ready to give up searching for a life partner. Some simply don't know how to go about finding a mate. Yet often they are limiting their own opportunities unnecessarily. Others believe that they don't match up to certain cultural stereotypes of attractiveness or sharpness and are convinced that they inherently lack the right stuff to find a compatible relationship.

Here I want to say as emphatically as I possibly can that you never have to reach this conclusion about yourself. What makes for attractiveness and, yes, sex appeal, has far more to do with your attitude and with how you manage your life than with those natural factors over which you have no control. To be sure, you can never become so successful socially that you are loved and accepted by everyone around you. Yet you can take certain steps and learn certain social skills which will greatly enhance the possibility of friendships and, ultimately, a marriage relationship developing.

When we examine the dynamics of friendships and romantic relationships, we find that there are certain qualities that commonly attract people to one another. Fortunately, these are qualities that you can learn, develop and improve upon to an important degree. There is an intangible factor in the chemistry that bonds two people together, admittedly; a relationship may take in one case but not another. Still, there are certain factors that can help your potential, in some cases considerably.

A passion for life. We are instinctively drawn to those persons who enjoy life and take a keen interest in their work and activities. If you want others to take an interest in you, do what you can to make yourself an interesting person. While you shouldn't repress the fact that you want a relationship, if your happiness and well-being hinge on finding one, you are in a self-defeating mode. Though the connection may not seem obvious at first, steps that you take to keep your life enriched and productive apart from a relationship will enhance the possibility of one developing.

Finding work which fits your motivational pattern, recreational activities which spark your creative interest, and other challenges which keep your life in a growth mode, will all increase your social prospects (if these activities don't become such obsessions that there is no time left for social life). As a general principle, you will be more likely to attract others when they sense your life is moving in a positive direction.

Common interests. It is intriguing to see how many romantic relationships begin between two people who share a common interest—a job or profession, a sport or hobby, involvement in a church or ministry project. I suspect, in fact, that most serious relationships begin this way. This again speaks to the need for an active social life but also to the importance of opting for activities that are likely to bring you into contact with compatible members of the opposite sex. Joining a men's baseball team or a woman's basketball team, for instance, will not increase your prospects as well as getting involved in a coed bowling league.

A passion for Christ. It is hard to overemphasize the impact which growing in Christ can have upon your potential for developing friendships and relationships. Though the effect is usually imperceptible in the short term, I've observed time and again that spiritual growth makes a person more attractive socially. Faithfulness to your daily devotions, to church and fellowship attendance, and to developing and using your spiritual gifts, will not only deepen your spiritual life but enhance your social life as well.

While I don't mean that God promises a mate to everyone who becomes a mature Christian, it is fair to say that spiritual growth will benefit you socially, through helping you become a more interesting person, through increasing your points of common interest with other believers, and through the intangible beauty that comes to a personality indwelt by Christ's Spirit. While this shouldn't be your primary motive for growing in Christ, neither should the point be neglected. Hebrews 11:6 enjoins us to keep the benefits of spiritual growth in mind as an incentive for deepening our relationship with God.

The Congeniality Factor

In his classic, *From Friendship to Marriage,* Roy Burkhart refers to a study made of one thousand married individuals, five hundred who were happily married and five hundred unhappily so. Each were asked to note the qualities which they found desirable in a mate. All, without exception, included congeniality.[1]

Congeniality refers to that range of social qualities that enable people to be friendly, supportive and encouraging to each other. To an important degree congeniality can be developed. Steps to increase your congeniality include:

Take an interest in the other person. Insensitive people bombard you with tales of their own experiences. Congenial individuals go out of their way to find out more about you and to identify with your interests. Especially helpful is the simple but important art of asking questions. Think through creative questions which you can inject in a conversation that will enable the other to share about his or her experience. Avoid questions which can easily be answered yes or no, but concentrate on those which will encourage the other to elaborate. For instance, ask: "What do you find most interesting (or most frustrating) about your work?" "What do you find most enjoyable (distasteful) about living in this area?" "Why did you decide to move here?" Ask questions like these and then relax and let the other talk! This is an art which even a very shy person can learn and master quite well.

Be affirming. Seek to give encouragement whenever and however possible. Look for little ways to compliment. Put the accent on affirmation, not criticism.

Be vulnerable. Let the other know your hurts and weaknesses, providing you are confident that he or she really wants to share this level of confidentiality with you. There is an art to doing this, to be sure. The goal shouldn't be to make someone feel responsible for your problems but to help the other feel a sense of common humanity with you. Carefully think through how you will articulate your personal struggles to someone else. Do so in a way that is sensitive to what he or she is ready to hear and that builds that person up.

Don't be argumentative. Resist the compulsion to always have to be right in a discussion. If you disagree with the other's opinion, do so in a way that shows respect for that person's judgment. Let that person know that while you see things differently, you don't have all the final answers, and you're grateful for the different slant on things which he or she is giving you.

Don't be touchy. In any friendship or close relationship there will be the need for forgiving and overlooking much humanness. Don't expect perfection. Don't be quick to conclude that someone's insensitive actions are meant as an affront to you; they may simply reflect idiosyncrasies or rough edges that spring from that person's upbringing. If confronting is necessary, do it in a way that is both self-effacing and affirming. Let him or her know that you also have areas that stand improvement.

Work on your sense of humor. It is amazing how closely many people associate a sense of humor with congeniality. While some are much more gifted at humor than others, all of us can work at seeing the lighter side of life and even at learning jokes to tell in appropriate circumstances. But be careful that your humor is not overdone or offensive to others. Jokes that poke fun at yourself, your own situation or background, are generally the safest bet.

The Physical Appearance Factor

Your physical characteristics are a gift of God. You have a unique mix of physical qualities which is exactly what is needed to accomplish God's purpose for your life. While cultural stereotypes of attractiveness abound, remember that in reality people differ widely in what they find attractive in the opposite sex. Some men are instinctively attracted to heavy women; there are tall women who are drawn to short men, and vice versa. Don't box yourself in or conclude that you don't have the right stuff physically simply because you don't fit a certain cultural mold.

Learn to think of yourself not in terms of one particular physical feature but as a unique combination of them. We tend to fixate on one aspect of our appearance which may concern us (such as height, weight, complexion, hair). Others, though, see you not in terms of that one feature but as a whole person—and not only a whole person physically but one with personality, talents, positions in life and other features that make up your personal uniqueness. When other factors in a relationship are good, many are amazingly flexible in revising their ideals about their partner's appearance. Again, don't lose your hope for a serious relationship simply because you fall short of some personal or social ideal of attractiveness.

In the survey which I referred to on page 184, there were only two factors which all one thousand individuals checked as essential in a mate. One, as we noted, was congeniality. The other was cleanliness.

How you care for your outward appearance makes a statement to others about how you view yourself as well as life in general. It also shows respect or lack of respect for others. By taking care of your grooming and dress, you show that you respect the fact that others are conditioned to appreciate the physical (Ruth 3:3). Taking care for your appearance is a compassionate move. If you simply say, "Someone must love me for who I am in spite of my lack of concern for appearance," you miss the fact that your physical appearance is part of who you are, part of the image of God within you. You need to show proper stewardship for it.

At the same time, obsession with this area is unnecessary. We are each beginning from a position of strength here. God has made each of us inherently attractive physically. You should think of grooming and dress as comparable to a frame around a painting; it should highlight the painting yet not overshadow it.

You may find it helpful to pick up a book or attend a seminar which gives guidelines for determining what colors best enhance your natural features.[2] Discovering which colors complement your attributes not only simplifies shopping and choosing your wardrobe but eases the strain on your pocketbook as well, for the right choice of color makes considerably more difference than the quality or cost of what you wear.

In the area of physical appearance the issue of weight is an obsessive concern for many. Frankly, I believe that far too much is made—even by certain Christian writers—of weight as a factor in finding a romantic relationship. A look around you and you see many happily married women and men who by popular standards are considerably overweight and were so at the time they married. There is nothing in Scripture or the Constitution which says that only those with a Miss Twiggy figure or the physique of a male model will be fortunate enough to find romance.

I find again and again that self-esteem plays a much greater role in sex appeal than the weight factor. If you are comfortable with your weight, and if you dress appropriately for your features, others will find you attractive. True, some who have stereotyped images in mind may judge you unfairly, but many will not. And some, as we've noted, are inherently attracted to those who break the stereotypes in this area.

My purpose isn't to discourage you from trying to lose weight, if you wish to do so, but to put the matter in sane perspective. Each of us should strive for the weight level that is most healthy—given our particular frame. Yet many of us will fall well short of perfection in this goal at many points in our lives. We can still have a positive self-image and present a personal image that is attractive to others. We can still enjoy friendships and quite possibly a marriage relationship.

You shouldn't, in other words, start with the premise that you will only be able to find a compatible partner once you reach a certain weight level. You can be attractive and have good social potential *now*. Work toward the weight level you want, but make the best of your present situation also.

When you are comfortable with your appearance, others will be also. As you learn to appreciate your physical attributes as God's gift and make a reasonable effort to care for them, you will have reason to be comfortable!

The Self-Esteem Factor

Self-esteem, of course, occurs on other levels besides the physical. Healthy self-esteem in any area is a plus in attracting friendship. This isn't to suggest that your self-esteem must be perfect to find a serious relationship. As with the weight issue, I think that too much is also made of self-esteem as a necessity for a successful social life. There are plenty of happily married people who have generally low self-esteem. Yet as you grow comfortable with the unique personhood which God has given you, others will be attracted to you as well. You should remind yourself constantly that God has made you distinctively, has given you gifts and qualities not imparted to any other person, and that he sees your life in an infinitely positive fashion.[3]

In recent years I've come to appreciate the influence of "self-talk" upon our self-esteem more. Psychologists point out that we talk to ourselves constantly, consciously and subconsciously, for good or ill, verbalizing our feelings, impressions and perceptions. If we've been programmed to think poorly of ourselves or to approach life in a self-defeating way, we are invariably speaking negative messages to ourselves much of the time. Often, though, these self-messages do not reflect the reality of our life as God sees it. Examples of negative self-talk include:

"She's prettier than I am."

"Everyone is looking at my outbreak of acne."

"People are thinking I'm a failure."

"I don't have what it takes to build a relationship with her."

As we begin to recognize the messages we are speaking to ourselves, we can slowly but surely work at changing these into ones which are more realistic and positive. The next time that you catch yourself feeling inferior or thinking your social prospects are nil, try saying to yourself: "God has made me unique. And he has made me attractive. Comparing myself to someone else is a case of apples against oranges. I determine to accept myself and appreciate myself as God has made me and to believe that I have exactly what is needed for him to work out his very best for my life."

The technique I'm suggesting is not just a bromide or a Band-aid approach to self-esteem but a process which over time can have a significant influence on your perceptions of yourself and your life. The important matter is to continue working at revising your self-talk until genuine improvement comes. The development of healthy self-talk takes time but is a realistic long-term goal.[4]

Your Availability

Statistics show that most people marry someone in close proximity to them—someone who lives near them, works with them, or whom they see frequently in some social context. This strongly challenges the popular notion that "absence makes the heart grow fonder," as well as the fantasy that God will bring the ideal mate to your doorstep even if you aren't socially active. Sociologist J. Richard Udry states it simply:

> It should surprise no one . . . that sociologists have consistently demonstrated that the likelihood of any individual selecting any given other individual as a spouse, other things being equal, is inversely related to the distance between their homes. (A recent researcher found the likelihood of marriage inversely related to the square of the distance—almost an exact parallel to the attraction of gravity and magnetism!) Surveys in dozens of American cities have revealed the same pattern of residence.[5]

While this presents a challenge, there is a wonderfully positive side to it as well: the mere fact of your availability may be the deciding factor (other things equal) that attracts someone to you. There is purpose in being active socially and in seeking those living, working and recreational situations where you are most likely to meet compatible individuals.

16
Praying for a Partner

This past week I had one of those wonderful serendipity experiences that from time to time comes in my study of Scripture. I was meditating on the first miracle of Jesus, his changing water to wine at the wedding feast in Cana (Jn 2). I've long been intrigued by the fact that he performed his first miracle at a wedding. It seems to symbolize his abundant willingness to bless all the particulars of bringing two people together in marriage. It reminds us, too, of the miracles he can work in that process.

Yet for the first time a thought occurred to me that will forever change the way I think about that passage: the miracle occurred in response to someone's *request.* We are given the strong impression that apart from the earnest urging of Jesus' mother, the six earthen jars would have remained so many empty vessels.

I am always moved profoundly by biblical examples of answered prayer. I include among my favorite passages of Scripture those which speak of God's response to petitions for a child. "And the LORD remembered her; and in due time Hannah conceived and bore a son, and she called his name Samuel, for she said, 'I have asked him of the LORD' " (1 Sam 1:19-20 RSV). And, "Do not be afraid, Zechariah, for your prayer is heard, and your wife Elizabeth will bear you a son, and you shall call his name John" (Lk 1:13 RSV). It never ceases to inspire me to think that God allows us to influence what happens in our lives not only through our actions but through our petitions to him as well.

Before looking at other steps toward finding a mate, it will be important now to look directly at the place of prayer. What should be its role in the process? I find that while some Christians hardly need to be exhorted to pray for a spouse, others greatly downplay the benefit which prayer might bring to their search for a life partner.

The Two Purposes of Prayer

Scripture speaks of two broad roles which prayer should play in our lives. The first is its effect upon us—its redemptive influence on our own disposition and outlook. Through prayer our attitude becomes more Christlike, we become more attuned to what God wants us to do and are generally encouraged as well. There are a variety of approaches to prayer which point us in this direction, from confession, to praise and thanksgiving, to meditation, to praying for the grace and strength to accept God's will as Jesus did in the Garden of Gethsemane.

Yet just as frequently, Scripture reminds us of the effect prayer has not only upon us but upon *God*. While the Bible never implies that we can manipulate God through prayer, it does emphasize that God purposely chooses to limit much of what he does in our experience to what we choose to pray for. He graciously extends to us the possibility of having influence through our petitions.

Of these two roles the first is clearly the most important. Our single greatest need as Christians is to stay in a relationship of trust with Christ where he can guide and encourage us. The benefits of a renewed heart extend to all areas of our life—inspiring health and vitality, the ability to enjoy our present situation, the capacity to think clearly about steps of faith which we should take.

The importance of the second role of prayer, though, should not be overlooked either. Through making requests of God we grow through taking responsibility and gain a valued sense of partnership in what he is doing. In his extensive study of prayer in Scripture, John Calvin concluded, "We see that to us nothing is promised to be expected from the Lord, which we are not also bidden to ask of him in prayers."[1] Scripture consistently shows, too, that the possibility of having influence through prayer is much greater than we normally think. The biblical emphasis on this point is so pervasive, in fact, that it led African pastor Andrew Murray to declare, "As image-bearer and representative of God on earth, redeemed man has by his prayers to determine the history of this earth."[2]

Practicing the Privilege

When it comes to seeking a partner for marriage, no one would deny the importance of prayer in keeping us grounded and encouraged in Christ. The obvious benefits are not only in this area but in all other areas of life as well. We clearly do well to give ourselves to the whole realm of prayer which Scripture recommends. But what about the second role? How important is it to *ask* God to bring about the possibility of marriage? I find that Christians generally have two hesitations here.

One is the fear that God doesn't want us to spend our energy praying over such a self-centered matter. Don't we do best to give our attention in prayer to more ministry-centered concerns?

There is no question that we need to pray faithfully for the needs of others and for broader concerns of Christ's ministry. Yet Jesus told us also to pray for our "daily bread," implying that we should give at least some attention each day to raising our personal needs to God. Paul made basically the same point in Philippians 4:6 when he declared, "Do not be anxious about anything, but in everything, by prayer and petition, with thanksgiving, present your requests to God." God, then, has encouraged us to be straightforward in bringing our personal needs before him.

More troubling for many, though, is the question of how bold and persistent we should be with the request for marriage. What if you've raised this request to God for months, years—or decades!—without receiving an answer? Doesn't the point come where you should cease your petition and simply pray for acceptance of your singleness?

The answer of Scripture is surprising. Jesus encouraged his followers to continue bringing requests to God until they received a clear answer. To this end he told two parables, one of a widow who continued to implore a judge to vindicate her case in court (Lk 18:1-8), another of a man who continued to ask a friend for bread to serve to an unexpected guest (Lk 11:5-8).

At first this seems brazen and irreverent, tantamount to pestering God. Yet in reality there are some vital benefits that come through long-term persistence in prayer. One is that our desires become clarified. When we persist in making a prayer over a period of time, we give God the fullest opportunity to work within us either to change our desire or to deepen our conviction that we really do want what we're asking.

In addition, persistence may be needed for the deepening of our faith. When we've only prayed briefly about a matter, we're likely to think an outcome has resulted from our own efforts or fortuitous circumstances. Long-term persistence in prayer deepens our conviction that God's help is needed and that he is behind the solutions that come.

It is striking that in both of the parables which Jesus told, someone persisted in asking help for a rather limited personal need. Certainly in a matter as life-changing and far-reaching as finding a marriage partner we should feel not only a license but something closer to a mandate to continue bringing the request to God.

Abusing the Privilege

This is not to say that praying for marriage cannot become an obsessive practice. It becomes obsessive if it either robs you of your well-being in Christ or diverts your attention from other responsibilities in prayer. A Christian woman in her mid-thirties who told me that she was continually depressed over being unmarried also admitted, "I spend a lot of time walking around my yard getting angry with God over my predicament." While I respect her honesty with God, I fear that her prayer life is doing more to hurt her than help her. In this case the second role of prayer is far overshadowing the first. Her ongoing argument with God about wanting to be married simply nurtures her frustration over being single. It does little to strengthen her contentment in Christ or to help her gain perspective.

A married friend of mine and his wife had a similar experience in praying about their infertility. He told me, "We made this a matter of constant prayer over a long period of time. After a while we discovered that our prayer life was little more than an attempt to try to jerk God's chain in order to get a child. Sure, our prayer life included adoration and intercession on behalf of others, but it was just preliminary measures to get to the real issue. Finally, we realized that daily, persistent prayer for a child was not only damaging the other aspects of our prayer life, but was also causing us to focus on this one matter in our daily activities. Our lives became consumed by this one issue."

Interestingly, they decided to stop praying for a child on a consistent basis. He notes that "after we made this decision I was able to focus more on communicating with God and growing in my spiritual walk with him. When my prayer life changed, I actually believe God gave me more insight into how I should approach the infertility crisis. I truly felt a wisdom from God about life in general that I'd not experienced earlier. My decision-making ability was greatly improved. And only then were we able to make some responsible decisions about our crisis."

My friend's experience brings us back to what the primary purpose of our prayer life should be—an activity which helps us to gain a joyful, Christ-centered perspective on our life. If you find that your prayers for marriage are working against you at this point, you should look carefully at why this is happening. It is possible you will do best to stop praying for this concern altogether, at least for a time.

More probably some adjustments in your prayer routine will solve the problem. Try giving at least half of your prayer time to praise, thanksgiving and devotional practices which strengthen your joy in Christ. And in the time spent making requests, give most of your attention to other concerns besides the desire for marriage. Spend significant time praying for the needs of others. Limit the time you devote to praying for marriage to two or three minutes at most. This should be quite adequate for expressing your concern, yet should prevent it from becoming the main focus of your prayer life.

Of course there may be exceptions to this pattern. If you're facing a major decision regarding marriage, then you may need to give more attention to this area for a time. But as a general rule, it is best to be persistent yet succinct in bringing regular petitions before God. Remember that most prayers of petition recorded in Scripture are brief and to the point. And many of them were far-reaching in their consequences.

Extended Prayer—A Special Privilege
There is, though, also an important place in Scripture for special times set aside for praying for special needs. The examples of Jesus in Gethsemane, Hannah in the sanctuary, Moses in the wilderness and many others remind us of the benefits that come from extended

prayer over a pressing need. The desire for marriage is often a justified reason for a personal retreat given especially to praying for this concern. Just be sure that praying in this fashion doesn't become an obsession. While taking a single or occasional personal retreat to pray for marriage is usually a good idea, doing so frequently is not.

To be honest, though, I seldom find that someone who wants to be married has ever spent an extended time praying for this need. My impression is that most Christians don't take praying on this level as seriously as they should.

My own experience, too, has given me reason to be optimistic about the benefits of such prayer. When I was twenty-six, I spent a day on a personal retreat for the purpose of asking God to provide a marriage partner for me. The time is vivid in my mind, for I picked a striking and beautiful setting for this time of prayer—the Blue Ridge Parkway and Skyline Drive route through central Virginia, as I drove home to Maryland from Roanoke.

It was about six months afterward that my relationship with Evie began, leading to our marriage a year later. I suppose I will only know in eternity if there was a relationship between that day spent in prayer and God's bountiful provision for my need. However, I suspect the connection was more than coincidental.

If you have never done so before, let me recommend setting aside a generous portion of time—an afternoon, a full day, a weekend perhaps, for the purpose of praying to God about your desire for a spouse. It is certainly not asking too much to give a day or two to an effort that may have lasting benefits. At the very least you should grow closer to Christ through the time. Beyond that it may open you more fully to his provision for your need.

Remember that such a time should not only allow you to express your desires to God but give him room to do his redemptive work within you as well. Be sure to plan your personal retreat with a view toward both of these goals. Give time to thanking God for his past provision in your life, especially in relationships: Pray for acceptance of your present state of affairs. Allow liberal time, too, for silent reflection. This is an opportunity for God to bring order to your thoughts and to help you see steps you may need to take to find an answer to your need.

But don't feel squeamish about clearly expressing to God your hope for marriage. Ask him to change your heart if in fact he doesn't want you eventually to marry. Yet be straightforward also in asking him to provide a partner for you within his own wisdom and timing. You will not force him to do anything he would not otherwise wish to do (Rom 8:26) but through this process will give him greater freedom to bring about his best for your life.

Whether in daily devotions or special times of prayer, we should take heart that God wants us to bring our petitions before him. The biblical message could hardly be clearer on this point. Before you make the effort to find a life partner, give some serious attention to praying for one. This could make all the difference.

17
Taking
Initiative

▰ ▰ ▰ ▰ ▰

When Abraham wanted to find a wife for Isaac, he faced no little challenge. Not only did she need to be from his own bloodline but someone spiritually and personally compatible with his son as well. This ruled out the women of the Canaanite community where he now lived.

So he did the logical thing. He decided to look in his former home region of Haran, convinced that the prospects of finding someone suitable for Isaac were good there. Since he was too old and infirm to make the journey himself, he delegated the role to a trusted servant.

When we think of this most beloved of romantic episodes in the Bible, we tend to remember what happened after this—how Abraham's servant sought God's guidance through prayer and was dramatically led to Rebekah. The story, which spans the longest chapter in Genesis (chap 24), profoundly underscores the role of prayer and faith in this remarkable sojourn.

Yet it speaks just as strongly to the initiative that was part of the process of finding Rebekah. And bold initiative at that. Abraham refused to be limited by his geographical confines, but went beyond them. And his servant displayed considerable courage in being straightforward with Rebekah and her family about his mission. Rebekah could have rebuffed him. And if her family didn't believe him, it could have meant his life.

The story, then, reminds us not only of the vital need for faith and prayer in one's search for a life partner but of the bold steps of faith that may be required as well. For Abraham seeking the right person for Isaac meant nothing less than some serious inertia breaking.

What might such inertia breaking mean for a Christian today? I want to look closely at that now. Some of the steps I'm going to recommend may seem scary to think about. They may increase the risk of being hurt, and they will certainly draw greater attention to the fact that you want to be married. Yet they may be exactly what is needed to put you in the best position to meet someone compatible or to allow a serious relationship to develop.

Be Open to Changing Your Circumstances

First, take a close look at the major circumstances of your life, including—

- ☐ your job
- ☐ your church situation
- ☐ fellowship groups in which you participate
- ☐ the community where you live
- ☐ community organizations, clubs, recreational or artistic groups to which you belong

Carefully consider two questions concerning each of these:

1. Does this situation provide a good opportunity for meeting compatible individuals of the opposite sex? A rural community, for instance, will not have the social opportunities which a metropolitan area affords. A small in-grown singles fellowship will not provide the benefits which a large and more transient group does. A job in which most of your associates are of your own sex has clear disadvantages.

2. Have you become stigmatized in any of these situations? In other words, do people think of you as a permanent single—a spinster or bachelor for life? Such stigmatizing occurs more frequently than you may like to think and can happen in the most congenial social situations. Generally it develops subtly. No one sets out to stereotype you, and often no one consciously realizes they have done so. Yet over time even the most open-minded individuals can form impressions of you which become difficult to change.

If, for instance, you have been involved in a singles group for several years and no one has asked you out, it is quite possible you have become stigmatized. It is also likely that you have stereotyped yourself, for we invariably absorb the impressions others have of us. If this is the case, you will do best simply to face the fact and move on to another group where you can begin with a fresh identity. Jesus himself had to relocate his home from Nazareth to Capernaum before his public ministry could flourish (Mk 2:1).

Carefully evaluate all of the circumstances in your life. Consider where changes, including major ones, can be made which will increase your prospects for meeting compatible people. Obviously it will not be feasible to make every change you might like to make. Yet be certain that the fear of what other people may think is not the only thing holding you back from a needed change. If it is, determine to see the change as a step of faith which God wants you to make. If you lose some approval from others in the process, so be it. You may gain far more in the way of social benefits on the other end. Remember that Ruth found Boaz only after making a major geographical move, from Moab to Bethlehem (Ruth 1).

I'm not recommending that you constantly jump from one situation to another in any area of life. Commitments must be honored, and if you have reason to know that God wants you to stay where you are, you must be faithful to that call. Yet if you have given a situation a reasonable opportunity and are not violating any trust by leaving, don't feel guilty for moving on. It is as justified to make a major change for the sake of finding a marriage partner as it is to further your career or educational opportunities.

During Brett's four years as an engineering major, he dated only a handful of times. Although he was eager to find a relationship which could lead to marriage, the prospects at the small college in his hometown seemed limited. Now graduate school provided the chance for a change—but would it be right? Friends and family urged him to continue his schooling at home, and he knew that his leadership role at the local church would be missed. Yet the state university several hours away not only provided education as adequate as his home college, but boasted a large campus fellowship group as well. This could be the environment in which to meet someone compatible for marriage.

The decision was a difficult one for Brett, and he finally gave a day to prayer and meditation over what to do. At the end of the day he concluded that while both alternatives were closely weighed, going to the state university seemed the more stewardly move, given his earnest desire for marriage.

During his first year there, he met Kelly through the campus fellowship, a woman who had come to the university from another state. A dating relationship developed, and they married upon Brett's graduation. Their marriage has been excellent, and even family and friends now concede that Brett's move to the state university was the right one.

I do want to say something more specific about the question of changing churches. Many Christians feel considerable loyalty to their churches and don't feel the freedom to leave simply for the sake of improving their social prospects. Such loyalty is commendable and, frankly, without a strong measure of such faithfulness from its members no church can long survive. A creative compromise, however, may allow you to remain at your church yet improve your options for meeting compatible singles.

In many communities, especially suburban and metropolitan areas, at least one church has a large singles group which includes many who belong to other congregations. In the Washington, D.C., area, where I live, the Ambassadors of Fourth Presbyterian Church is a dynamic singles fellowship of about five hundred which welcomes those who are active in other churches. Excellent marriages, far too many to count, have come from relationships forged through this group. Three of the last four weddings which I've officiated, in fact, have been for couples who met through this group. Many who attend Ambassadors meetings on Thursday evenings or early Sunday mornings also maintain active membership elsewhere. Fourth Presbyterian is very accepting of the arrangement and makes no effort to proselytize them away from their home churches.

I encourage you to look for such a group in your own area. You may be surprised to find that one or more exists. Phone churches within driving distance of your home, ask other Christians for recommendations, and search the religious sections of newspapers for ads and pertinent announcements. It is quite possible you can find an arrangement that will allow you to attend a good singles fellowship but maintain your commitment to your home church.

If this isn't possible, you may need to look at changing your membership to a church which provides a better opportunity for meeting suitable singles. While it can be very difficult to think of leaving a church where your roots go deep, remember that you cannot be all things to all people. The priority of finding a mate is an important enough reason to make this change.

Seek the Support of Others
Be tactful but honest in letting friends, family members and other

sensitive individuals know of your desire to find a spouse. Ask them to pray for you and to keep their eyes open for you. Many good marriages come through referrals of this sort.

In *Beyond Cinderella* Nita Tucker suggests having a support group of individuals who agree to take a special interest in helping you find a partner.[1] Though I have never heard this suggestion made in Christian circles, I think it is an excellent one. Select three to six trusted individuals who care for you and ask them to come to a group meeting. Explain to them that you wish to be married but are having difficulty meeting compatible people. Ask them if they will carry this concern with you and meet with you from time to time to talk and pray about it. Ask them if they will make it a priority to be alert to opportunities for you. And set some specific dates for future meetings, perhaps at one-month intervals.

The encouragement that comes through this sort of arrangement can be remarkable. And it significantly increases the level of support which others give you, for members of such a group tend to encourage each other to be diligent in the task of helping you find a relationship.

Be Open to Those of Other Races

A woman who managed an introduction service for Christians in my area told me that of several hundred who filled out her questionnaire, only a handful checked that they were open to marrying someone of a different race. I'm certain that this is one of the most unfortunate restrictions which we place upon ourselves in looking for a spouse. I am aware of many fine marriages between individuals of different races or cultures. Your best opportunity for finding a spouse may be with someone from a race or social context other than your own. Remember that one of the most impressive individuals in the New Testament, Timothy, was the child of a mixed marriage (Acts 16:1). God is not limited to monocultural arrangements in bringing about good marriages for his children.

Don't Live with Your Parents

Singles who continue to live with their parents into their twenties and
beyond, regardless of the motive, imply to others that they have not
truly broken the apron strings and thus lack the maturity for marriage.
While this is not always a justified perception, it persists nonetheless.
You will best maximize your chances by establishing an independent
home, living either by yourself or with other singles of your sex.

Computerized Dating Services

Christians are generally indisposed to taking advantage of professional services for matching compatible people. While we are comfortable
with this concept in other areas of life (such as seeking career opportunities), we are not in the area of making social contacts. Yet when
we consider the fact that historically both parents and professional
matchmakers (*shadkhan*) played a significant role in arranging He-
brew marriages, we cannot say that this approach is inherently against
the will of God. God can and does use any means at his disposal to
bring about his will for individuals, including technology and specially
trained persons.

I agree with Christian sociologist Herbert Miles, who in *Singles, Sex
and Marriage* stresses the value of professional introduction services.
He notes:

> I heartily approve socio-marriage agencies that are run by respon-
> sible Christian people for the purpose of helping singles meet
> marriage prospects. . . . Of course, young people of college age do
> not need such an agency when there are dozens of prospects all
> around. But older singles—the never-married, widows, widowers or
> divorced—often need, and thousands of them would welcome,
> anonymous help in finding a marriage partner. . . . There is noth-
> ing unsocial or unchristian about meeting a prospective marriage
> partner through a social organization that uses the blessing of
> modern technology. A marriage agency is not trying to play Cupid.
> It only introduces people. The processes of courtship and all final

decisions are made by the persons involved.[2]

Carefully consider Miles's arguments before you discount the possibility of seeking help from a professional service. I would personally encourage you to take advantage of the best resources available to you in finding a mate. If there is a matchmaking service in your area which has a reputation for integrity, and if the fee is not outrageous, avail yourself of it. I know a very impressive missionary couple who met through a computerized service while in college. They have been married about fifteen years now and have had an exemplary marriage.

Often we rule out the viability of professional dating services because of the bad reputations gained by some of them. Yet we don't discount the importance of church ministry simply because many local churches are ineffective. The concept of professional assistance in finding a spouse is a good one. Be open to using such assistance if it is available.

Break the Ice

Be sensitive but bold in initiating contact with someone whom you are interested in getting to know. Regardless of your experience or success with relationships in the past, realize that you may have the particular mix of qualities that will appeal to this person. You will never know unless you try.

Let me say that I empathize with the most extreme fears you may have about initiating a relationship. I was so desperately shy as a young teen-ager that it took me five full months from the time I first decided to phone a classmate for a date until the evening when I finally—and just barely—mustered the nerve to do it. The most outrageous fears held me back. I imagined her laughing at me, telling me I was out of line for phoning her and pictured myself stammering speechless on the phone. I'm embarrassed to admit how many hours and evenings were invested in aborted attempts to make a phone call that I never could complete.

My experience also demonstrates how utterly out of sync with reality our visions of failure often are. When I finally did phone her, her response could not possibly have been more affirming. She not only accepted the date, but told me enthusiastically that she had been hoping for some time that I would ask her out. A dating relationship began which lasted for over a year. It was a good, healthy relationship, which nurtured us both in many important ways.

Yet I remember so well how I came within a hair's breadth of not making that one phone call which paved the way for an important relationship and proved my fears to be the straw men which they were. In the end it was this one step of initiative that made all the difference. Had I not made the call, I would have gone on assuming that a relationship like this was not in the cards for me.

In the years to come I was to experience some disappointments in relationships as well; I was not always as successful as on this first occasion. But I can say honestly that I have never in any instance regretted making the attempt to begin a relationship. Even when my hopes have not been realized, I have always learned from the effort.

If you have the opportunity to initiate a relationship, don't let unreasonable fears hold you back. Whatever your reasons for hesitating, realize that there are undoubtedly much better reasons for going ahead. Honestly, what do you have to lose? A small dose of pride, perhaps, if the answer is no. Much to gain if the answer is yes. Even if it is no, you will grow through the process and strengthen your courage for future encounters.

Go ahead and break the ice. Take a step on the cutting edge of faith, and trust the Lord to give you all the grace needed in the process.

18
Should a Woman
Take
Initiative?

◆▬◆▬◆

Frank and Linda have a secret. They've only shared it with a few trusted friends during their ten years of happy marriage. It's not that they feel ashamed about it—quite the contrary. But they do fear that some in their church wouldn't understand.

The secret is that Linda proposed to Frank.

Well, at least sort of.

"Linda was the first to suggest getting together," Frank admits. "And I'm so glad she did. I was so uneasy around the opposite sex that I blushed just seeing a woman's picture. After several awkward conversations at church, she asked if I'd come to her home one Sunday afternoon to watch the football game."

"I did pick up the ball from there," he points out. "Her making that first move did wonders for my courage, and I began to call her every night. But at several points when I got scared and stopped phoning, Linda had to jumpstart our relationship. She got me talking again and helped me realize that I really did want the relationship to continue."

"Finally she had to courage to say what I hadn't been able to bring myself to say. She told me that she would like to spend the rest of her life with me. I'll tell you, I sure picked up the ball after that. A week later I took her to a classy restaurant and formally proposed as we were eating the main course. I thought she'd get us kicked out for the shouts of joy that came out of her mouth! It was just wonderful. But I really have my doubts I could have reached this point with a less assertive woman than Linda. I'm eternally grateful for her taking the initiative that she did."

Challenging the Custom

Frank and Linda's marriage has clearly worked well. And Linda's initiative in bringing their marriage about is only too clear. The question is whether Linda acted within the bounds of Christian propriety in taking this initiative. Have God's blessings come *because* of her initiative or *in spite of it*?

I know that for many readers this question is much more than an academic one. Many Christian woman, faced with the reticency of so many Christian men, would like to feel the freedom to take the sort of initiative which Linda did. And many others, frankly, would greatly improve their prospects if they did.

Yet Christian women face a double constraint here. Traditional Christian thinking, with its emphasis on male headship and authority, has frowned upon women playing anything but a quiescent role in initiating relationships. It is generally regarded as out-of-place for a woman to take such basic steps as phoning a man for a date or even suggesting in a casual way that they get together. Her role is to wait passively and prayerfully and leave it to the man to do the pursuing.

Though there has been some rethinking of this point in evangelical circles in recent years, the traditional emphasis remains strong.

Our secular culture, too, does not make it easy for a woman at this point and at best sends her mixed signals. While the feminist movement has proclaimed emphatically that a woman should feel free to play any role she wants in a relationship, there are still strong currents of traditional thinking within our society. Depending upon where you grew up, the attitude of your parents and friends, you may have been strongly admonished to leave the initiating to the man. It is fair to say that the belief that a woman should wait demurely for her prince to come still prevails in more segments of our culture than not.

Many assume that these attitudes of our Christian and secular cultures originate in Scripture. In reality, though, when the Bible is carefully examined on the point, it is found to present a different and much more liberating perspective. While it has plenty to say about women (as well as men) being respectful and not pushy in relationships, it says nothing against a woman being the initiator at important stages of a relationship. To the contrary, in the most elaborate description of a courtship in the Bible, that of Ruth and Boaz in the book of Ruth, it is Ruth who takes the initiative to let Boaz know she is open to marriage with him (Ruth 3). While she is not at all brazen, neither is she squeamish about putting herself in a position in which Boaz will have no doubts about her hopes.

Nowhere else does Scripture forbid a Christian woman from taking the initiative to begin a serious relationship or from taking the lead in talking about the direction of the relationship or the desire for marriage itself. As a matter of principle, she should certainly feel the same level of freedom at these points which a man does. Our uneasiness with this perspective, I'm convinced, springs from cultural conditioning and not from sound biblical understanding. Here I agree heartily with Christian sociologist Herbert J. Miles, who insists that a single Christian woman "has a right to take the initiative by correspondence, telephone, or personal contact to meet and become acquainted with any person she is interested in knowing better."[1]

Miles not only observes that Christian women should have this right, but he notes that there are often distinct advantages to their exercising it:

There are several benefits when women take the initiative. It could mean an end to some long, lonely evenings and weekends. Her initiative would give her a wider selection. It could mean more marriages. Since women tend to look more deeply than just physical attractiveness, they are more likely to find a more compatible mate. Female initiative would tend to produce better marriages. The courtship role is key to planning marriage and life. Nature and society have thrust upon women the responsibility of child-bearing and much of the responsibility of the home. Surely the woman should have the right to choose a life companion who would be meaningful to her across the years.[2]

There is a further reason why it is often a good idea for a woman to take initiative. More often than not she is more comfortable socially than the man, who may even be considerably shy. It only makes sense for her to be the first one who opens up. Apart from her initiative, the relationship may never get off the ground. Frank and Linda's relationship is a classic case in point.

Exercising Discretion

Of course saying that it's O.K. for you to take initiative and saying that you should do so in every case are two different things. My purpose in saying that it's permissible is not to have you commit social suicide! Unquestionably there are men who would be offended if you made the first move. Here you simply have to pray and make a judgment call. If the man whom you wish to get to know seems shy, chances are he will greatly appreciate your being straightforward about getting together. I can testify that as a shy single, I was grateful and never offended on several occasions when a woman took such a step with me.

You might suggest that you have lunch together after church or go out for ice cream in the evening. Keep the situation low-key and low-budget, so the question of who should pay does not become a big issue. Be ready to pay for both of you or for yourself, but if he offers and seems earnest, allow him to cover it.

Yes, you do run the risk that he will not take well to your assertiveness. Yet if he is very shy, chances are he will never get around to contacting you anyway. There is simply no way to remove the element of risk in initiating relationships.

Be open to initiating a second casual get-together if necessary. During that time be clear in telling him that you would like to see him again and would enjoy hearing from him. After that it is probably best to wait and allow him to make the next move. While it may be necessary with an extremely shy man to continue initiating things for a time, most men will feel comfortable and affirmed enough by this point to contact you if they wish to further the relationship.

You may find, though, that with a shy or socially inexperienced man it will be necessary to take initiative again from time to time at certain transition or crisis points in your relationship. Again, Frank and Linda's relationship is a typical example. Linda needed to draw Frank out several times when he was ready to put things on the shelf. In these instances Linda understood Frank's feelings better than he did, and her sensitive initiative saved the relationship. And if Linda had not finally suggested the idea of marriage, she might still be waiting for Frank to pop the question.

On the other hand, if the man whom you wish to become acquainted with is fairly comfortable socially, then it may be wisest to let him make the first move. While you should be clear in letting him know that you would like to get to know him better, you may do best to make some casual suggestions and let him pick up the reins from there. Statements like "I really enjoy talking with you" or "I hope I'll get more opportunity to see you" may give him all the cueing he needs. If, after a month or two, there has been no follow-through on his part, then it certainly would be in order for you to suggest getting together for lunch or a casual date. Pray and use your best discretion.

Whether or not you decide to take initiative in a relationship, remember that biblically you do have the right to do so. And if you have this right, then this just might be where taking a step in faith would more fully open you to God's provision. Be open to that possibility, especially if things are at a standstill in your dating life and have been so for some time.

Yes, there is risk involved. But (must I say it?) nothing ventured nothing gained. As Linda's experience reminds us, sometimes there is much to be gained through such a step of faith.

19
Dealing
with
Rejection

▲▲▲▲▲

I've spent two weeks crying over losing him."

So Louise described to me her reaction to being shelved by Harold. Louise is not a self-pitying person, but a mature, vivacious Christian woman. Yet she was much less prepared for what happened than she thought. She had let her hopes get too high about a relationship with Harold. And not without good reason. Harold had said he was open to the possibility of a serious relationship. But after several months he decided that their differences on certain doctrinal matters were too great. They would do best to forgo getting serious but stay friends.

Friends? Small comfort to someone who has had marriage in mind.

I remember thinking as a new believer that Christians must be fairly well insulated against major heartbreak. I was to find in time, as Louise has, that our humanity remains well intact. It is something that even the most stouthearted among us discovers. Rejection cuts deep.

We come now to a matter that is not as pleasant to think about or anticipate as others we've looked at. Yet it is an area of experience that is just as essential to understand and be prepared for if you are to realize your goal of finding a lifetime companion. That fact is that you will probably go through at least one experience of rejection or disappointment on the way to meeting the person you should marry.

I originally considered entitling this chapter "Accepting the Inevitability of Rejection." I decided against it because it is too negative and connotes a sense of fatalism about rejection which I don't mean to imply. I want this book to boost your hopes, not diminish them.

Still, that title does capture something of what I want to say. If you are to stay appropriately hopeful about finding a partner, you have to be steeled for the sort of experiences that too easily squash your dreams. Far too often a single episode of rejection is enough to do this. For many, too, the mere fear of the possibility of rejection alone is enough to keep them from moving off square one. In either case the reaction is much more extreme than warranted. Indeed, rejection, rightly understood and dealt with, can take you closer to your goal of marriage rather than further away. It is not the ultimate catastrophe we make it out to be.

The truth is that I don't know any happily married person who didn't go through at least one major disappointment before finding the person who was right for him or her. Most went through several unhappy episodes prior to meeting their spouses. It's not that this absolutely has to be the case. Yet it doesn't seem that God exempts many of us from this pattern.

None of these persons will deny that the pain of these disappointments was considerable. Yet most will also admit now that there was positive value in even the most difficult relationship experiences in the past. These not only helped prepare them for the realities of marriage but sometimes in ironic ways brought them closer to meeting the person who became their lifemate.

Seeing Rejection with the Eyes of Faith

With the right perspective it is possible not just to survive rejection or the unhappy ending of a relationship but to actually benefit from the experience. It all has to do with your perception. Typically, when disappointment occurs in romance, we are prone to three unfortunate conclusions:

1. "I am unlovable." I don't have the right stuff for someone to love me in a marriage-quality way.

2. "God doesn't want me to be married." He has shown me through this closed door that he wills for me to stay single.

3. "I won't be able to love again." The one person whom I truly loved is not available. It would be ungenuine to think that I could feel this same intensity of love for another person.

Each of these conclusions is unnecessary and tragic—unnecessary in that it doesn't likely reflect the reality of our life as God sees it; tragic in that if it persists, it too easily becomes a self-fulfilling prophecy. This becomes clear as we look closely at each of these.

I Am Unlovable

We are instinctively prone as humans to reason from the specific to the general. When the emotional intensity of an experience is great, we tend to view the rest of life through the eyes of this one experience. Yet the conclusions we draw can be most misleading.

It is not exaggerating things to say that the death of expectations for a relationship can be as heartbreaking as the physical death of a loved one, especially when you have placed great hope in these being realized. In *Coming Apart* family therapist Daphne Rose Kingma suggests that the ending of a relationship of short duration can be even more painful than that of a long-term one, for there has been less chance to see the other's imperfections and thus to have some basis for seeing value in the breakup.[1] Of course, the failure of a relationship even to get off the ground can be devastating if your hopes have run high about it. The rejection of a single date can be enough to crush you.

In the wake of any such experience of loss, there is grief which must be experienced and worked through. It is normal to feel at a very low point at such a time and to dwell on your disappointment. At this point, though, while not denying your feelings of disappointment, you must make every effort to remind yourself that this relationship was but one among an almost infinite variety of possible others for you and that it does not have to mirror the reality of things for your future. In the immensely complex world of romantic relationships, where the chemistry does not take in one case it takes wonderfully and surprisingly in another. There are so many intangible and unpredictable factors involved in what draws two people together that you never have a basis for concluding that all future hope for a good relationship is gone.

Beyond this is the very important fact that you can often learn valuable lessons from failed relationships which will improve your prospects for finding an enduring relationship in the future. I say this cautiously, for it is not always true that you can learn clear lessons from past failures, and you must be careful of self-flagellation in the process. My advice is to look only for very obvious lessons which can be learned.

In my own case, for instance, I learned through two difficult experiences as a young Christian that women found me insensitive when I spoke too soon. I told them early in the relationship what I thought to be God's will for our future. As I came to understand how presumptuous I was being in doing this, I determined to change the pattern. It allowed for a much more relaxed and spontaneous relationship with Evie.

Let me caution you, though, to avoid with determination the thought that things might have turned out better if you had acted differently. There is simply no way to know this. Here you need to rest fully in grace and the protective hand of God to trust that he has your very best in mind in what you've gone through. Even if you had done everything perfectly, the breakup might still have occurred. As painfully academic as the thought may seem at this time, the day may come when you thank God from your heart that things transpired as they did. When you've met the right person, the relationship will work in spite of many weaknesses and imperfections on your part.

In any case, don't fall into the trap of predicting your future on the basis of your past. Your past experience in relationships in no way proves what your future experience will be. Someone else may respond to you very differently. Don't write history before it happens!

God Doesn't Want Me to Be Married

When we experience romantic disappointment, we tend to reason outward from that one experience to what broader message God might be giving us about our life in general. Too often the conclusion we reach is a negative one: God is showing me through this roadblock that I should stop pinning my hopes on getting married and should face the reality that he wants me to stay single.

Seldom, though, is this conclusion justified. When Paul speaks to the issue of how to set your heart concerning marriage (1 Cor 7), he simply says that you should plan on getting married if your need is strong. Obviously, he realized that some of his readers did not immediately have a prospective spouse and that some had been rebuffed in their efforts to find one. Yet never does he remotely suggest that the lack of present opportunity or any number of past failures should be taken as indicating that God is telling you not to plan on getting married.

Quite the contrary, he even says that widows should look toward getting married again if their need for marriage remains strong (1 Cor 7:8-9; 1 Tim 5:14-15). I doubt that anyone is more inclined to conclude that God doesn't want them married than the one who has suffered the death of a spouse. Yet Paul allows no room for such a fatalistic assumption. Underneath it all, his attitude is supremely optimistic.

Why, then, does God allow us to experience disappointment in relationships if the reason is not to show us that we should plan on staying single?

One very important reason is to keep us from entanglements which would not be good for us. In his infinite knowledge of the future God sees much more clearly than we possibly can whether a particular relationship would result in a healthy marriage and contribute to his best intentions for our life. "There is a way that seems right to a man, but in the end it leads to death" (Prov 14:12). Sometimes the only way God can protect us from the romantic equivalent of driving off a cliff is by bringing about the breakup of a relationship that we cherish. Only with time and hindsight do we appreciate the wisdom of his action.

Another reason is to teach us lessons about life and relationships which can only be learned through experience. Also, difficulties build tenacity and resilience into us which can only be acquired through experience. Such events bring us back more fully to trusting him to meet our deepest needs.

Finally, but not least significantly, there is a more mystical factor that can be often demonstrated but never fully explained. There seems to be a law in life that a certain number of failures are sometimes required to bring about a success. To say it differently, success sometimes comes only through a number of earnest attempts. It is the principle of seed bearing which is talked about so frequently in Scripture. Some seeds take root while others don't, for reasons we never fully understand. Yet the greater the number sown, the greater the likelihood of a rich harvest. Thus Scripture declares,

> As you do not know the path of the wind, or how the body is formed in a mother's womb, so you cannot understand the work of God, the Maker of all things. Sow your seed in the morning, and at evening let not your hands be idle, for you do not know which

will succeed, whether this or that, or whether both will do equally
well. (Eccles 11:5-6)

When disappointment comes in romance, our tendency is to think
that failure once means failure forever. We see the lots cast against
us and imagine ourselves living an isolated, lonely life. Yet the principle of seed bearing suggests that an experience of failure may indicate that we're now in line for a success as much as anything.
Success isn't less likely now but more so! If we'll simply keep casting
the seeds, eventually one will take root.[2]

It's fair to think of this, too, as a principle of compensation. Failure
with one try is compensated for by success at another. All of this adds
up to one important point: There is purpose in trying again when you
experience disappointment or rejection in a relationship. You must
not close the door in this or any area of your life before God is ready
to do so.

I Won't Be Able to Love Again

Even if you accept that you might be successful in another effort,
though, you may find it hard to imagine that your feelings of love
could be redirected to someone else. Hasn't God so created us that
full-bodied romantic love can only be experienced for one person in
a lifetime?

As pervasive and deep-seated as this notion is, it hits wide of the
mark of reality. In fact, God has so constructed the human psyche that
the feeling of romantic love can be experienced toward a potentially
large number of persons. He has put within each of us a remarkable
measure of resilience. It is to this end that Paul tells the widow that
she "is free to marry anyone she *wishes*" (1 Cor 7:39, emphasis added).
Clearly underlying the statement is the assumption that the widow will
be *able* to love again. If this is true for someone whose spouse has
died, it certainly can be true for those who have experienced a broken
relationship.

It is noteworthy that Boaz is Ruth's *second* husband, her first having died in Moab. Ruth is once again able to invest her romantic energy. It is in the book of Ruth, too, that God is described as "a restorer of life" (Ruth 4:15 RSV). This is a vital concept of God to keep in mind in the face of disappointment. He is a God who heals, and a significant part of his healing work involves enabling rejected individuals to find new directions for their affection. Thus, the remarkable description: "A father to the fatherless, a defender of widows, is God in his holy dwelling. God sets the lonely in families" (Ps 68:5-6). And Psalm 113:9: "He gives the barren woman a home, making her the joyous mother of children" (RSV).

This is not meant to minimize the excruciating pain involved in any experience of rejection or to say that the pain should be expected to pass quickly. But it is to say that there is light at the end of the tunnel. Over time the pain can be overcome and romantic affection redirected.

I experienced these feelings of rejection when a friend in my college fellowship told me politely but firmly that she wasn't interested in dating me. I had let my hopes get out of hand about a relationship with her and was feeling quite shot down. I confided in a pastor friend who advised that while I shouldn't ignore my feelings of disappointment, I should move as quickly as possible to find a new place for my affection.

He expressed the point in symbolic terms: "If you have a glass filled with dirty water, there are two ways to get it out of the glass. You can dump it out, in which case the dirty water is quickly gone but the glass is left empty. Or you can take a pitcher of clean, cool water and begin pouring that into the glass. Gradually the fresh water will displace the dirty water."

He went on to explain that the empty glass represents the unhealthy way of dealing with a broken relationship: bailing out of life, turning off your emotions, turning a hard heart to the possibility of new relationships. Pouring fresh water into the glass represents the healthy approach. You admit the feelings of regret, which are only too real, while at the same time taking steps to build new social contacts. Gradually the new life that comes from these will take the place of the anguish which now seems so overpowering.

His advice proved sound. Within a week I found the courage to ask out another woman in the fellowship, and the experience was surprisingly uplifting to me. My hurt feelings continued to gnaw at me for some time. But new friendships, and eventually marriage itself, brought substantial healing. Even today it's possible for me to jog myself back into the feelings of that hoped-for relationship of some twenty years ago. But I can also say with gratitude that I'm glad now that it didn't work out.

Symbols are important to us, and I believe you will find the metaphor of the pitcher and the glass a helpful one to keep in mind in the face of disappointment in relationships or any other area of life. God has built great resilience into each of us. We are much more capable of rebounding from rejection and failure than we may realize. Yet there is an important process involved, and this analogy says it as well as any elaborate explanation could. Don't let the inertia of life overtake you when things don't turn out as you had hoped. Break the inertia, seek new relationships and new outlets for your energy, and let the cool water fill the glass.

Rejection, while always a painful experience, does not have to be a catastrophic one. Indeed, when rightly responded to, it can be a positive step toward your goal of finding a good and lasting relationship. "We know that in all things God works for the good of those who love him, who have been called according to his purpose" (Rom 8:28). "All things" includes rejections and unwanted endings to relationships. Even in these he is working out a plan that has your very best in mind. Dwell on that as you seek his courage to move forward.

V
Confronting
the Fear of
Commitment

20
Understanding the Fear of Commitment

▲▬▲▬▲▬▲

Whlle the fear of rejection keeps many from taking steps toward marriage, others are hindered by a quite different apprehension—the fear that they might be too successful. They dread the thought of being locked into a binding relationship, with all the responsibility, trappings and loss of freedom involved. It's the fear of commitment, not the fear of rejection, that holds them back.

Often those who fear commitment do long for the benefits of an intimate relationship. Yet the thought of losing freedom so frightens them that they experience considerable conflict within and often display erratic behavior. An approach/avoidance pattern results, which is bizarre to anyone who doesn't understand the nature of the fear;

such persons move toward intimacy at one point in a relationship, away from it at another.

Normal Jitters

Some apprehension in the face of a step as momentous as marriage is not only normal but healthy. Not to feel at least some fear is to indicate that you have neither appreciated the element of risk involved nor weighed the cost carefully enough. No matter how carefully the decision is approached, any thinking person realizes that a decision which will radically affect the rest of life is being made on the basis of very little information. No decision forces you to confront more fully the frailty and limits of your own thinking.

There is, too, a normal process of grieving as you face up to the loss of personal freedom involved in getting married. No matter how greatly you long to be married, there is sacrifice involved. While the trade-off in a good marriage is always much more than worth it, still there is grief over what you are giving up to become permanently attached.

When Marjorie agreed to marry Ted, she was strongly confident that she had made the right decision. As their wedding day approached, however, she became increasingly apprehensive. What if she had made the wrong choice? What if Ted turned out to be a different sort of husband than she imagined? What if she found marriage to be too confining?

Wisely, Marjorie sought advice from a counselor. After reviewing her reasons for deciding to marry Ted, the counselor assured Marjorie that she had made an excellent choice. He told her, too, that her fears were quite normal and understandable and that she would be wisest not to let them hinder her from going ahead with the wedding.

Marjorie left the session relieved. Up till this point she had assumed that when God leads a person to marry, no doubts or fears intrude. Now at least she was no longer afraid of her fear, for she realized she wasn't abnormal for having some apprehension. Though she continued to feel some jitters up to the day of the wedding, she went ahead with it and afterward felt immense relief. It was clear now that she had to take this step simply to put her fears to rest. She and Ted have been married for nine years now, and she has never wavered in her confidence that she took the right step.

The type of doubts and apprehensions which Marjorie experienced during her engagement period are so common that they are the rule and not the exception for those who take a mature approach to marriage. They are part of the adjustment process involved in making the momentous leap from singleness to a lifetime commitment. Most people, when they come to understand how normal it is to have these fears, are able to deal with them, rise above them and move on to marriage. And most, like Marjorie, find that once the vows have been taken, their fears vanish. Until that point there was always the opportunity to change their mind, and knowing that made them prone to reanalyzing their decision. Now, with the final bridge burned, they are able to feel a degree of confidence they hadn't known before.

Don't Fence Me In

For some, though, the fear of commitment takes on a more serious dimension than this. For them it is nothing short of a phobia. When the fear of commitment reaches this level, it truly interferes with their ability to do what they most desire or believe is best. It is not enough for them simply to be told that it is normal to be fearful or to be assured of Christ's protection, for their level of discomfort is so great they can only think about getting immediate relief from it.

I identify with the problem of irrational fear, being a white-knuckled flyer. No amount of consoling statistics or exhortation to trust the Lord frees me from my dread of flying or the sense of entrapment that comes once I'm on board an aircraft. As I once described it for a magazine: "I don't want to say that I dislike flying. I'll simply say that I'd rather have my appendix out without an anesthetic than go up in an airplane. Yes, I know all about statistics. You're safer in a plane than in a car—the whole bit. Such statistics are cold comfort to me when the terra firma's no longer so firma. In the air all I can think about is becoming a statistic. Frankly, I'd prefer you just don't mention the word flying around me."[1]

My fear is an irrational, disabling one resulting from many learned emotional and physical responses which are hard to undo. For one who is phobic about commitment, the dynamics of the fear are much the same, only the object of fear is different. This person may greatly enjoy dreaming about the possibility of marriage (just like I can indulge pleasant fantasies about flying when a trip is not impending). And this person may strongly desire the benefits of marriage (just like I want the marvelous advantages of travel which flying provides). Yet when faced with the imminent reality of commitment, this person panics and feels the same claustrophobic entrapment which we phobic flyers experience once the cabin doors slam shut.

Though this may sound overdramatized, I can assure you that for some the fear of commitment is this severe. Like all phobias, though, the fear of commitment comes in varying degrees. For some it is strongly debilitating, for others only mildly so. I find it most helpful to think in terms of four levels at which the fear of commitment commonly occurs.

Level One—The Screeching Halt

Eric courted Ellen relentlessly for five months, getting only indecisive replies. Finally, as they were driving home from a singles' retreat, Ellen said that she had had time that weekend to think it over and that, yes, she would like to be his wife. Eric was so overjoyed that he nearly drove the car off the road.

Yet the next day Eric seemed unusually cold and distant when he phoned Ellen at her office. He explained that an emergency had come up at work, and he would have to work late the next several evenings. Each time they spoke on the phone that week Eric seemed jittery and anxious to get off as quickly as possible. Though perplexed, Ellen wrote it off as work stress.

Then the bombshell. When Ellen arrived home Thursday evening, a note from Eric was taped to her apartment door. It read, in part: "I've come to realize that I made a big mistake in thinking we should get married. The Lord has shown me this week that it isn't his will for us to be together and may not be his will for me ever to be married at all. The reasons are deeply personal and have nothing to do with you at all. I'm really sorry, as I know I got your expectations up. Yet I know nothing will be gained by talking about this. Let's just trust this to the Lord and move on."

All attempts to contact Eric in the weeks that followed were either unsuccessful (he made himself as unavailable as possible) or unproductive (he was cold and refused to talk about their relationship). Finally, mortified and bewildered, Ellen gave up, assuming she must have made some terrible mistake which turned Eric against her.

Though Eric's behavior following Ellen's acceptance of his offer of marriage seems incomprehensible, it is a more common response than many realize.[2] His discomfort rose to such a level that he could only think of escaping. Ellen was left shaking her head wondering what she possibly did to provoke him. In reality, Eric left not because the relationship was bad but because it was *good;* nothing Ellen could have done—short of refusing his proposal—would have prevented this.

Often persons with extreme commitment fear desire the benefits of an intimate relationship as long as the pressure of a binding commitment is not there. Frequently, too, these persons imagine that they really do want a permanent relationship. Usually it is security needs that trick them into such a deluded mindset. They need to know their partner will commit to them for the sake of their own self-esteem.

Yet once they know that the other will commit—and expects them to be committed—they panic. Because their fear of being locked into a relationship is greater than their desire for a relationship, they want out. When this fear reaches the level which Eric experienced, they can only think of breaking free as quickly and completely as possible. This accounts for (but of course does not excuse) the brutal and insensitive way in which commitment-phobic persons sometimes break things off. Their anxiety runs so high that they cannot think of the other's needs but only of their own need to break free.

Level Two—On-Again, Off-Again

There is another level of commitment fear which, while less extreme than Eric's, is still quite debilitating. It is epitomized by the on-again, off-again response.

During the two-and-a-half years that Andy and Melissa dated, Melissa agreed no less than five times to marry him, including two formal engagements. Within a day to a week following each of these acceptances, she would be plagued with severe doubts and, with great embarrassment, would tell Andy that she couldn't go through with marriage at that time. Yet never did she want to break up with him. Each time she begged him to give her more time to sort through her feelings and make a decision. And in time she always came back to a point of conviction and told Andy with considerable confidence that she would marry him. But within a short period the doubts intruded again, and Melissa broke things off.

Though a remarkably patient person, Andy finally reached his limits and broke up with Melissa. Yet during the year since, Melissa has continued to intimate that she would like to get back together with him and is open to discussing marriage. Andy continues to wonder if he is being too harsh and if it's reasonable to expect that in time Melissa will not only agree to be his wife, but actually walk the aisle with him.

As with Eric, Melissa's fear of commitment is greater even than her desire for a marriage relationship. Yet it is not so great that she feels compelled to flee the relationship altogether when commitment-panic sets in. Rather, she takes steps to keep the relationship intact while freeing herself of any immediate obligation to the future.

Once the immediate pressure of commitment is off, she begins to feel comfortable in the relationship again. In this state she begins to dream again of the advantages of marriage and starts to imagine that she can overcome her fears just by trying a little harder. Given the right inspirational setting—a Sunday-afternoon canoe ride or a candlelight dinner—she warms to the idea of marriage to the point of wanting to commit, and she does so with confidence. Yet once reality sinks in, her fears overrule and the pattern repeats.

Level Three—Ongoing Ambivalence

For some the fear of commitment is about equal to their desire for marriage. Sam's relationship with Rebecca demonstrates this well. They have dated over three years. They have talked often about marriage and have spent long hours dreaming together about what it would be like to have a family, a home and a life dedicated to one another.

Rebecca has been quite up-front in telling Sam that she would like to be his wife. Sam has told Rebecca that he loves her more than anyone he has known, that he knows she would make a fantastic wife and that he cannot imagine being married to anyone but her. Yet Sam, an impressively honest man, has consistently added that the thought of a binding forever-type commitment frightens him. At the same time, he has pleaded with Rebecca to be patient and to give him time to grow out of his fears. He doesn't want to lose the prospect of marrying her.

Rebecca, who also cannot imagine being married to anyone other than Sam, has continued to cherish the hope that he will eventually come around. Yet after three years, her patience is wearing thin, and she wonders if she's wishing for the moon. Though Sam has remained quite faithful to her, there hasn't been any clear evidence that he will ever change.

Because Sam's fear of commitment is not as extreme as Eric's or Melissa's, he is less prone to repress it and thus less prone to the erratic behavior which they fell into. In other words, because he is more aware of his fear and more upfront in dealing with it, he is less likely to make a commitment which he can't keep in the first place.

Yet Sam demonstrates a pattern which is common at this level of commitment fear: long-term inertia in a serious relationship. The relationship stays serious, there is much talk and loving dreams about the possibility of marriage, but it always stays in the realm of possibility. The moment of decision is never reached. Sam loves Rebecca and longs eventually to marry her. Yet *eventually* is the key to his attitude, for if it gets any closer than this, he freezes. He is like the person with a moderate fear of flying who longs to visit family members in a distant city and dreams often about it but can never take the final step to purchase a ticket and make the flight.

Relationships like Sam and Rebecca's sometimes go on for years, until the fearful one finally overcomes his or her inhibitions enough to break the inertia and make a commitment, or the other person finally gives up and bails out. There is greater hope that the persons at this level of fear can eventually get beyond their inhibitions and make a meaningful commitment than there is for those at the first two levels. Yet it often requires an extreme measure of patience, understanding and sensitivity on the other's part, which, understandably, some are unable or unwilling to provide.

Level Four—Normal Apprehension

Finally, as we've said, there is a level where commitment fear can actually be termed normal—even healthy and non-threatening—provided it is properly understood. At this point one's desire for marriage and intimacy is greater than one's fear of commitment. Yet, as we noted in Marjorie's case, some fear persists nonetheless, due to humility about the limits of one's own knowledge and the process involved in letting go of old attachments to take on a new and more greatly desired one. Such fear, in right proportion, indicates that you are taking the decision seriously and working through the necessary adjustments involved.

The danger is that you may overreact to being afraid. This will especially be true if you assume that unbending confidence must always accompany any decision led by Christ. In that case you'll be inclined to take your uneasiness as a red flag to the decision to get married.

Like Marjorie, when most people are helped to put their apprehensions in right perspective, they are able to accept them and get beyond them. These don't end up being the hindering force which fears of the more phobic nature tend to be. To the contrary, apprehension at this level actually benefits them, for it moves them to a greater dependence upon Christ and to appreciate the marriage decision more fully as the step of faith which it always must be.

21
When the
Problem Is
Your Partner's

▲▲▲▲

How can you know if the one you're dating, or thinking of dating, is fearful of commitment? Is there a way to spot this before it becomes a problem in your relationship?

Your partner may be up-front in admitting to you that he or she is apprehensive about commitment. Yet until you know someone very well, you cannot count on that person being completely honest about areas that might jeopardize their chances in the relationship. Also, it is the nature of this fear, particularly at the more extreme levels, that it tends to get repressed, especially when one is not immediately faced with the prospect of commitment. Your partner may not recognize the existence of the problem, or may think that a past episode of it was an aberration from his or her true character. Yet, unless this person shows clear evidence of change—usually requiring professional help—you shouldn't assume that a past demonstration of commitment fear was an aberration. The chances are high that the pattern will repeat again.

Looking at your partner's past history in relationships will give you important clues about his or her attitude toward commitment. You have a right to be suspicious if your partner has:

☐ Abruptly broken off a relationship in the past shortly after committing to marriage.

☐ Demonstrated an on-again, off-again pattern in a past relationship.

☐ Broken off two or more relationships at some point after committing to marriage.

☐ Been involved in three or more serious relationships which extended for two years or more without being able to resolve whether to marry. (I'm not speaking here of situations in which someone else broke up with your partner or was the one who couldn't decide about marriage but in which your partner was the ambivalent one.)

To be sure, it's possible that your partner's past behavior resulted not from commitment fear but from an unrealistic perspective on God's guidance. He or she may have been expecting an unreasonable sign from God to confirm the marriage decision or may have been waiting for an impossible measure of inner certainty. It's also possible that your partner was harboring unreasonable ideals about a romantic relationship. Your partner may have modified his or her expectations and be in a better position now for a healthy relationship. If either of these is true, and if your partner has had a genuine change of perspective, then you shouldn't hold past behavior against him or her. This person deserves another chance.

But if there is no clear evidence that your partner's behavior resulted from problems of perspective, you can assume that this person is fearful of commitment. If your relationship reaches the commitment stage, the chances are strong that the pattern will repeat.

Keeping the Windows Closed

You should be *highly* suspicious if your partner is overly secretive about his or her life. It's common that those with extreme commitment fear will keep important windows of their life closed to those whom they date. One reason is the fear of getting too intimate with anyone. Another is the fear that the one whom they're dating will find out too much about their past relationships. In addition they may be concerned to keep their escape routes open. The less their partner knows about the particulars of their life, the easier it is to disappear.

To be more specific, you have good reason to be uncomfortable with anyone who after several dates:

☐ Doesn't want to introduce you to their parents.

☐ Doesn't want you to visit their home.

☐ Is uncomfortable with you ever visiting them at work, phoning them at work or knowing much about the particulars of their work.

☐ Introduces you to none or few of their friends.

☐ Only wants to be alone with you; consistently avoids any opportunity to be together with you in the company of their friends or business associates.

☐ Doesn't reveal specifics about trips they make—or gives dishonest or misleading details about them.

Taking Control

Of course, determining that someone is fearful of commitment and deciding what to do about it are two different matters. If you are comfortable with the thought of having a serious relationship with someone which may not end in marriage, then, of course, you are justified for staying in the relationship—only guard your heart.

If you are one who likes to court risk, you may want to try your hand at helping this person get beyond his or her commitment fears. Perhaps you have the gifts and disposition needed to help this person toward healing. It is very unlikely, though, that someone at a level one or two commitment fear will be healed without professional help. You must accept the fact that your role will probably amount to convincing this person to get the professional counseling needed. Remember, too, that in the midst of your optimism you must keep your feelings in check; the chances are good that your partner will never be able to commit to you. You must be prepared for any outcome.

You are also quite justified in breaking off a relationship with someone who is fearful of commitment, just as you are justified in avoiding the relationship in the first place. This is not being uncompassionate (assuming that you handle things sensitively) but simply is part of being a good steward of your life. Remember that Christ has told us that we are to be not only gentle as doves but wise as serpents in our dealings with people (Mt 10:16). This principle must apply as much to the realm of romantic relationships as any other.

Too Close for (Your Partner's) Comfort

But what if your relationship is already at a serious stage and your partner has displayed one of the patterns I've described? First, let me say something about a level one response. If (heaven forbid) someone has abruptly broken off a relationship with you shortly after agreeing to marry, has been insensitive, distant or untalkative since and seems to have undergone a personality change, you can rest assured that he or she is a classic commitment-phobic.

You are probably at your wit's end right now wondering what you did wrong or what you can possibly do to repair this tragic breach. It is vital that you understand that the relationship aborted not because of what was wrong but because of what was right. Your partner suffers from a severe fear of commitment, and it is very unlikely you will be able to change this. Though it seems very cold for someone to say this, you will do best to abandon hope that this relationship will ever work out and move on.

Most importantly, do not blame yourself for what happened. Learn what you can from this dreadful experience and keep your guard up against it happening again. But remember, too, that most people are not as severely phobic about commitment as this. Don't harden yourself against the possibility of trying again with a more stable person.

It sometimes happens that a person who abruptly and insensitively breaks off a relationship after committing to marry comes back weeks or months later and asks for another chance. With the threat of commitment now removed, what once attracted that person to you is now attracting him or her again. They may plead with you to give them another opportunity and may insist (yes, even with tears) that they will not treat you as they did before. It may be very tempting to give in.

Remember, however, that even though on the conscious level this person may be quite sincere, he or she has already demonstrated a serious lack of self-understanding in committing and then abandoning you before. What evidence is there that this person's self-understanding is any better now? You should only agree to a renewed relationship if he or she has either undergone a successful program of counseling to deal with the fear of commitment or is clearly willing to do so. Even then, you should guard your heart carefully until you have proof that your partner has actually grown in his or her ability to handle commitment.

Perhaps, though, you're in a relationship with someone whose fear of commitment is more of the level two type. If your partner has made a commitment to marry you and retracted it two or more times, yet still wishes to stay in the relationship, you need to look carefully at the reasons for this pattern. As we've noted, an on-again, off-again pattern can result from an unrealistic perspective on guidance (expecting unreasonable confirmation from God) or from holding onto unreasonable ideals. If, however, there is not some clear point of perspective that accounts for his or her erratic responses, or if your partner is not able to revise his or her perspective, again I must be a wet blanket in saying that you are in a futile situation as far as the prospect of marriage is concerned.

If you have the patience of Job, if you can tolerate your partner's inconsistency, and if you are able to accept the possibility of not marrying this person, then you have reason to maintain the relationship. With this level of commitment fear, however, your partner will only be likely to get beyond it with professional help.

But what about a level three situation—that is, the long-term relationship that never reaches the commitment stage, even though both express much interest in marriage? This is the situation of commitment fear that I encounter most frequently among older singles. Here I'm comfortable giving you a rule of thumb for determining whether in fact level three commitment fear is present. If you both are into your mid-twenties or beyond, your relationship is well into the second year or beyond and one wants to marry but the other can't decide— even though he or she strongly desires to maintain the relationship at a serious level—then it is probable that this person has at least a moderate fear of commitment. Again, the exception would be if there is some clear issue that is keeping him or her from being able to decide. If the issue is addressed, yet they still cannot resolve to marry, commitment fear is probably the cause.

Here you must make a judgment call, and you are frankly justified either for staying in the relationship or not. It is possible that if you bear with this person, your patience, sensitivity and tenacity will in time be used by the Lord to help them over the hump of indecisiveness. You must steel yourself for the possibility that this will never happen. Yet because this person's fear of commitment is about equal to his or her desire for marriage, there is a reasonable possibility that desire will eventually prevail over fear. It is also possible that this person can be persuaded to get professional help. Someone at this level of commitment fear is more likely to be open to it than those at levels one and two.

Getting Outside Help

Be aware that the same fear which makes your partner apprehensive about committing to marriage may cause him or her to be uneasy about the commitment and intimacy involved in regular counseling sessions. Though he or she may promise earnestly to seek help, don't be surprised if there is no follow-through. It may take the most extraordinary gentle persuasion skills you can muster to get your partner off dead center on this one.

If you have resolved that you will only stay in the relationship if your partner faithfully seeks help, then you should set the following minimum guidelines:

1. He or she should seek out a pastor, psychologist, psychiatrist or professional counselor who is skilled in treating phobias and who understands the dynamics of commitment fear. While it is always nice if the counselor is a Christian, it is not absolutely necessary that this be the case if he or she is at least respectful of your spiritual stance. Because the need is for healing from a specific fear, not the broader concern of gaining perspective on life itself, you do best to get help from someone who understands the dynamics of phobias. (In the same way I wouldn't hesitate to recommend that you go to a non-Christian surgeon for removal of a ruptured appendix, if that person was the best one available to perform the operation.)

Finding the right person may take some shopping around. You can begin by asking your pastor for references, but don't hesitate either to ask for recommendations from your physician or local hospital. If you are not certain about the ability of a given counselor to help you, interview him or her with your partner and ask clear questions about that person's experience with this type of problem. In the end you will have to make a judgment call about the capacity of a counselor to meet this need.

2. Once you have found a qualified counselor, it will be important for both you and your partner to meet initially with him or her, together or in separate meetings, to get a clear perspective on what course of therapy needs to be followed. The counselor will probably suggest that your partner agree to an approximate number of sessions (perhaps ten). It will be important for you to know this and to be aware whether your partner is actually following through with these.

3. When the process is complete, you should meet with the counselor by yourself and get a clear evaluation as to your partner's progress.

If your partner objects that all of this amounts to you breathing down their neck too much, or if your partner tries to skimp on some of these details, you can conclude that they are not as serious about overcoming the fear of commitment as they need to be to justify your staying in the relationship. When the fear of commitment is at level two or above, authentic healing will require bold moves on both your part and your partner's. It is understandable if you don't want to get involved to this extent. But you should not count on miracles happening apart from this, any more than you should expect someone with a physical disease to get better without professional help.

Yes, the Lord can intervene and heal directly, and he does do this. He can do it with phobias as well as with physical problems. But you shouldn't be the one left with the burden of having to determine if healing has really occurred. If your partner has been erratic in his or her commitment in the past, the burden should be on that person to demonstrate conclusively that he or she is beyond putting you through this torture again. It is not asking too much that someone with professional counseling skill help in determining this and, if necessary, assist with the healing process.

22

When the
Problem
Is Your Own

◆◆◆◆◆

But what if fearing commitment is my own problem? How can I take steps to deal with it?

Perhaps you already knew that you are fearful of commitment, or perhaps you've begun to suspect so as you've read the discussion so far. If you're not certain whether you are, let me advise you simply to look at your past history in relationships.

Have you had a relationship in which you desired marriage but then lost interest once the other became willing? Now that the relationship is over do you look back with some regret and feel that in a sense you sabotaged a good situation? Have you been in a relationship in which you've fallen into an on-again off-again interest in marriage—wanting it, but then getting frightened and backing off each time a commitment was made? Have you been in a long-term relationship in which you wanted to marry and the other was clearly willing, yet you could never bring yourself to the brink of a final decision? Have you had several relationships that follow one or more of these patterns?

Again, it is possible that your ambivalence sprang more from problems of perspective than from fear. You may have been expecting God to tell you in some dramatic way that you have found the right person; or you may have been cherishing unreasonable ideals about what that person should be like. Perhaps the discussion in this book has helped you work through to a more healthy perspective and you are in a position now to move into a stable relationship.

Yet if there seems to be no clear point of perspective at fault here, the chances are strong that you are suffering from some unhealthy commitment fear. If so, then I cannot urge you strongly enough to seek professional help. Your resistance to doing this may be strong. We tend to ignore the severity of a phobic problem when we do not immediately have to face the objects of our fears (I feel little anxiety about flying, for instance, when a trip is not scheduled in the near future). Yet it is important for you to realize that your problem is a serious one. Your fear is doing nothing less than keeping you from something that underneath you do greatly desire. You want many of the benefits of a serious relationship and of marriage itself. But fear of losing your freedom and of being locked in is putting you in a self-defeating mode, causing you to neurotically destroy chances for success that come along.

Please understand that I'm not suggesting there is anything wrong or subhuman about staying single, if that is what you really want to do. Singleness is a gift of God and a joyful lifestyle for those who are inherently inclined toward it. Yet here my concern is for those who stay single not because they truly want to but because of unhealthy apprehensions about marriage being too confining. Here the biblical pattern is that we should address our fears and gain mastery over them, rather than give in to their control. Our constant temptation in the Christian life is because of fear to acquiesce to a level that is less than our full potential in Christ and thus to fall short of what we are most genuinely motivated to do.

Dealing with Normal Apprehension

As we've noted, some fear is normal in taking a step as major as marriage. Some fear is actually healthy, for it gives you over to the reverent attitude needed for entering a lifetime commitment. It is healthy *if* it doesn't paralyze you or cause you to walk away from a good opportunity for marriage. If you have made a commitment to marry, or are on the verge of doing so and are experiencing fears of the manageable type, you probably don't need professional help in dealing with them (though it certainly won't hurt to seek encouragement from a pastor or counselor). What you most need is assurance that you're not abnormal for having these fears and that they don't by definition mean that you've missed the leading of God in your decision.

You may also find it helpful to take a short personal retreat. Get away by yourself to a pleasant, reflective setting for a day or so. Thoroughly review your reasons for marrying this person. If, in this meditative environment, you feel confident about your choice, then go ahead and don't let normal nervousness dissuade you.

Put your trust in the absolute sufficiency of Christ to protect you and even redirect you, if perchance you have made the wrong choice. Then determine to put your hand to the plow and not look back.

Remember, too, that most of our anxiety about the future results from worrying about how we might cope with given problems. Scripture promises, though, that God will give us exactly the grace we need to deal with each contingency of life. While this principle underlines all of Scripture, it is stated most expressly in my favorite verse of the Bible: "And from his fulness have we all received, grace upon grace"

(Jn 1:16 RSV). The Greek literally states "grace following grace," implying a continual flow of grace, or more specifically, fresh grace every split second of our existence! Yet it is characteristic of grace that it's never given until the very moment needed. Our anxiety results from trying to predict exactly how God will give grace for a problem. But we can never know this until the moment comes. We can only know that when the moment arrives, the grace will be there. This is why Jesus urged us to live each day unto itself (Mt 6:34).

This perspective on grace is perhaps the most important thought you can keep in mind as you move toward marriage, with the multitude of uncertainties ahead of you. Most of the problems you worry about will not occur. Yet if they do, God's grace will be more than sufficient for your moment of need.

Christ intends the Christian life to be an adventure. Our greatest happiness and our greatest fruitfulness come when there is a reasonable measure of adventure in our life. Frankly, our modern evangelical teaching stresses the security part of Christianity too much, whereas Scripture lays much more emphasis on the adventure involved in walking by faith. While God does meet important security needs through marriage, I'm certain that the adventure side of it is even more important in his design of human life. Once we accept that adventure is *supposed* to be involved in a step of faith, that step becomes easier to take and the challenges seem less intimidating.

If the thought of moving toward marriage frightens you, think of it as an unparalleled opportunity for adventure.

Dwell on that thought.

And dwell on the protection and grace which Christ promises to provide you.

With those assurances in mind, go ahead.

Take the plunge.

And may God be with you and uphold you each step of the way.

Notes

Chapter Two: Does God Want Me to Be Married or Single?

[1]Rhena Taylor, *Single and Whole* (Downers Grove, Ill.: InterVarsity Press, 1984), pp. 6-7.

[2]Ibid., p. 7.

[3]Such as Paul's exuberant view of marriage in Ephesians 5:21-33. The relationship of husband and wife is compared to nothing less than that of Christ and the church.

[4]Ray C. Stedman, *Body Life* (Ventura, Calif.: Regal, 1972), p. 56.

[5]C. Peter Wagner, *Your Spiritual Gifts Can Help Your Church Grow* (Ventura, Calif: Regal, 1979), p. 63.

[6]Herbert J. Miles, *Singles, Sex and Marriage* (Waco, Tex.: Word, 1983), pp. 147-50.

Chapter Three: Is God a Matchmaker?

[1]By Donna Walters and used by permission.

[2]I realize that the phrase in this verse, translated by RSV "to take a wife for himself," is rendered in two other ways by other translations: "to gain mastery over his body" (NEB) and "to guard his member" (NAB). I am following the conclusion of O. Larry Yarbrough, who devoted a major portion of his Ph.D. thesis to examining 1 Thessalonians 4:3-8, that the RSV translation is the most reliable one. See O. Larry Yarbrough, *Not Like the Gentiles: Marriage Rules in the Letters of Paul* (Atlanta, Ga.: Scholars Press, 1985), especially pp. 68-76.

Chapter Four: How Can I Know God's Will?
[1]See my *Knowing God's Will: Biblical Principles of Guidance* (Downers Grove, Ill.: InterVarsity Press, 1979), pp. 78-82.
[2]Nita Tucker with Debra Feinstein, *Beyond Cinderella: How to Find and Marry the Man You Want* (New York: St. Martin's Press, 1987), p. 57.
[3]For those who wish to do a more in-depth biblical study of this issue, in the appendix of *Knowing God's Will*, pp. 127-34, I examine exegetical issues related to authority relationships for parents, spiritual leaders and spouses.
[4]Michael Harper, *Prophecy: A Gift for the Body of Christ* (Plainfield, N.J.: Logos, 1970), pp. 26-27.

Chapter Five: Can I Be Certain?
[1]Charlie W. Shedd, *How to Know if You're Really in Love—Really in Love Enough for Marriage* (Kansas City, Mo.: Sheed, Andrews and McMeel, 1978), p. 2.

Chapter Six: Do You Feel Deep Compassion for the Other Person?
[1]Jim Conway, *Men in Mid Life Crisis* (Elgin, Ill.: David C. Cook, 1978), p. 187.

Chapter Seven: Are You Good Friends?
[1]Quoted in *Newsweek*, "How to Stay Married," August 24, 1987, p. 54.
[2]Sol Gordon, Ph.D., *Why Love Is Not Enough* (Boston, Mass.: Bob Adams, Inc., 1988), p. 38.
[3]Ibid., pp. 38-39.
[4]Ibid., p. 36.
[5]Larry Richards, *Remarriage, a Healing Gift from God* (Waco, Tex: Word, 1981), pp. 23-24.

Chapter Eight: Are You Both Ready for Marriage?
[1]Maurice Lamm, *The Jewish Way in Love and Marriage* (San Francisco: Harper and Row, 1980), p. 8.
[2]Howard M. Halpern, Ph.D., *Cutting Loose: An Adult Guide to Coming to Terms with Your Parents* (New York: Bantam, 1976).
[3]Since Halpern is not a Christian author, you will not be likely to find his book in a Christian bookstore. In a few places he expresses some perspectives on lifestyle that differ from Christian attitudes. Most of his perspective, though, is quite compatible with Christian thinking, and the book on the whole offers a redemptive and compassionate approach to adult relations with parents. Unfortunately, I don't know of a Christian book to recommend which compares with it.
[4]See for example, Brenda Schaeffer, *Is It Love or Is it Addiction? Falling into Healthy Love* (New York: Harper/Hazelden, 1987); Stanton Peele with Archie

Brodsky, *Love and Addiction* (New York: Signet, 1975); Howard M. Halpern, Ph.D., *How to Break Your Addiction to a Person* (Toronto: Bantam, 1982); Drs. Connel Cowan and Melvyn Kinder, *Smart Women, Foolish Choices: Finding the Right Men, Avoiding the Wrong Ones* (New York: Signet, 1985); Robin Norwood, *Women Who Love Too Much: When You Keep Wishing and Hoping He'll Change* (New York: Pocket Books, 1985).

As with most psychological and self-help books written by non-Christian authors, you will find ideas in each of these that conflict with Christian values. Each book, though, does have valuable insights into the nature of addictive love and practical steps that can help you overcome your vulnerability to unhealthy relationships.

Chapter Eleven: Are You Spiritually Compatible?
[1]I draw on material here from the appendix of my book *Knowing God's Will*, pp. 130-31.

Chapter Twelve: Are You Emotionally Compatible?
[1]I borrow the term *motivational pattern* from Ralph Mattson and Arthur Miller who employ it in their books: *The Truth about You: Discovering What You Should Be Doing with Your Life* (Old Tappen, N.J.: Revell, 1977) and *Finding a Job You Can Love* (Nashville: Thomas Nelson, 1982), see especially chapter six.

[2]Hans Walter Wolff, *Anthropology of the Old Testament* (Philadelphia: Fortress, 1974), pp. 65, 96.

[3]I explore this point in much greater depth and provide many biblical examples in *One of a Kind: A Biblical View of Self-Acceptance* (Downers Grove, Ill.: InterVarsity Press, 1984).

[4]The procedure I recommend here is similar to that recommended in Mattson and Miller, *Finding a Job,* and Richard Nelson Bolles, *What Color Is Your Parachute? A Practical Manual for Job Hunters and Career-Changers* (Berkeley, Calif.: Ten Speed Press, 1984), pp. 83-86.

[5]Paul Tournier, *The Healing of Persons* (New York: Harper and Row, 1965), p. 67.

[6]Keep in mind that these are objective and not judgmental descriptions of personality. Melancholic, for instance, doesn't imply melancholy but an analytical and deep-thinking attitude. You will find a thoroughgoing and readable discussion of these four types in O. Hallesby's classic *Temperament and the Christian Faith* (Minneapolis: Augsburg, 1962) which is available in many public libraries. Paul Tournier also has a helpful discussion of these in *The Healing of Persons,* chapter 6, also available in public libraries.

Chapter Thirteen: Are Your Expectations Compatible?
[1]Robert L. Mason and Caroline L. Jacobs, *How to Choose the Wrong Marriage*

Partner and Live Unhappily Ever After (Atlanta: John Knox, 1979), pp. 18-23.
[2]Smith, *Knowing God's Will*, pp. 78-82.

Chapter Fifteen: What Will Attract Someone to You?
[1]Roy A. Burkhart, Ph.D., *From Friendship to Marriage: A Guide to Youth in His Search for Friends and a Life Mate* (New York: Harper and Brothers, 1937), p. 75.
[2]One helpful resource is Carole Jackson, *Color Me Beautiful: Discover Your Natural Beauty through the Colors That Make You Look Great and Feel Fabulous* (New York: Ballantine, 1973).
[3]In *One of a Kind* I look extensively at the issue of self-esteem and present a biblical basis for accepting your own distinctiveness. Refer to that book if you want to do further study in this area. Bruce Narramore, *You're Someone Special: "God Isn't Mad at You"* (Grand Rapids, Mich.: Zondervan, 1978), and Joan Lloyd Guest, *Self-Esteem* (Downers Grove, Ill.: InterVarsity Press, 1984) are also excellent resources.
[4]For further study, read Shad Helmstetter, *The Self-Talk Solution: Take Control of Your Life—With the Self-Management Program for Success!* (New York: Pocket Books, 1988).
[5]J. Richard Udry, *The Social Context of Marriage* (Philadelphia: J. B. Lippincott, 1974), p. 156.

Chapter Sixteen: Praying for a Partner
[1]John Calvin, *Institutes of the Christian Religion*, 3.20.2.
[2]Andrew Murray, *With Christ in the School of Prayer* (Old Tappan, N.J.: Revell, 1974), p. 103.

Chapter Seventeen: Taking Initiative
[1]*Beyond Cinderella: How to Find and Marry the Man You Want.* As is the case with many books by secular authors on marriage decision, this one contains some helpful advice along with perspectives which are not compatible with a Christian lifestyle. If you choose to read this book, you will want to do so with discretion.
[2]Miles, *Singles, Sex and Marriage*, pp. 123-24.

Chapter Eighteen: Should a Woman Take Initiative?
[1]Miles, *Singles, Sex and Marriage*, p. 118.
[2]Ibid., pp. 118-19.

Chapter Nineteen: Dealing with Rejection
[1]Daphne Rose Kingma, *Coming Apart: Why Relationships End and How to Live through the Ending of Yours* (New York: Fawcett Crest, 1987), p. 71.

[2]Other biblical examples include Genesis 26:19-22; John 21:1-8; Acts 16:6-10.

Chapter Twenty: Understanding the Fear of Commitment
[1]Blaine Smith, "Fear of Flying," in the "Leaps and Bounds" column of *HIS Magazine,* February 1983, p. 26.

[2]Steven Carter documents numerous instances of the screeching halt response among men he has known and interviewed in his popular book *Men Who Can't Love: How to Recognize a Commitment-Phobic Man before He Breaks Your Heart* (New York: Berkley Books, 1987). I do not generally recommend this book, since Carter deals only with this extreme level of commitment fear and doesn't give attention to other levels at which it occurs. The book, too, is long on analysis and very short on cure. Additionally, I disagree with Carter's insistence that extreme commitment fear is only a serious problem among men. While it is most common with men, I find it occasionally to be a problem with women as well.

About the Author

Blaine Smith, a Presbyterian pastor, is director of Nehemiah Ministries, a resource ministry based in the Washington, D.C., area. His work includes giving seminars, lectures and conferences. He also counsels and writes. He has authored two previous InterVarsity Press books, *Knowing God's Will* and *One of a Kind* (on Christian self-image) and for seven years authored the "Leaps and Bounds" column for InterVarsity's *His* Magazine.

Blaine is a graduate of Georgetown University and also holds a Master of Divinity from Wesley Theological Seminary and a Doctor of Ministry from Fuller Theological Seminary. He lives in Damascus, Maryland, with his wife Evie and their two sons, Benjamin and Nathan.

You Can Receive Blaine's Newsletter
Blaine authors a monthly newsletter, "Nehemiah Notes." It lists his activities and always includes one or more articles on topics such as knowing Christ and keeping a grace-centered perspective in requesting it (it is supported by voluntary gifts from readers).

To request Blaine's newsletter or to correspond with him, you may write:

Nehemiah Ministries
P.O. Box 448
Damascus, Maryland 20872

115033